LEARNING OBJECTIVES F~~OR:~~

MANAGING QUALITY CUSTOMER SERVICE

The objectives for *Managing Quality Customer Service* are listed below. They have been developed to guide the user to the core issues covered in this book.

The objectives of this book are to help the user:

1) **Learn how to set quality service standards**

2) **Identify characteristics of a winning customer-service team**

3) **Explore proactive customer-service problem solving**

4) **Understand customer-service audits and feedback**

Assessing Progress

Course Technology has developed a Crisp Series **assessment** that covers the fundamental information presented in this book. A 25-item, multiple-choice and true/false questionnaire allows the reader to evaluate his or her comprehension of the subject matter. To buy the assessment and answer key, go to www.courseilt.com and search on the book title or via the assessment format, or call 1-800-442-7477.

Assessments should not be used in any employee selection process.

MANAGING QUALITY CUSTOMER SERVICE

William B. Martin, Ph.D.

A Crisp Fifty-Minute™ Series Book

This Fifty-Minute™ book is designed to be "read with a pencil." It is an excellent workbook for self-study as well as classroom learning. All material is copyright-protected and cannot be duplicated without permission from the publisher. *Therefore, be sure to order a copy for every training participant by contacting:*

THOMSON
COURSE TECHNOLOGY

1-800-442-7477 • 25 Thomson Place, Boston MA • www.courseilt.com

MANAGING QUALITY CUSTOMER SERVICE

William B. Martin, Ph.D.

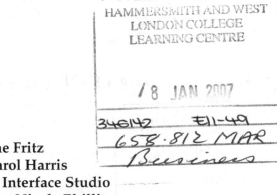

CREDITS:
Editor: **Elaine Fritz**
Designer: **Carol Harris**
Typesetting: **Interface Studio**
Cover Design: **Nicole Phillips**
Artwork: **Ralph Mapson**

For more information contact:

Course Technology
25 Thomson Place
Boston, MA 02210

Or find us on the Web at **www.courseilt.com**

For permission to use material from this text or product, submit a request online at www.thomsonrights.com.

Trademarks
Crisp Fifty-Minute Series is a trademark of Course Technology. Some of the product names and company names used in this book have been used for identification purposes only, and may be trademarks or registered trademarks of their respective manufacturers and sellers.

Disclaimer
Course Technology reserves the right to revise this publication and make changes from time to time in its content without notice.

ISBN 0-931961-83-1
Library of Congress Catalog Card Number 88-92732
Printed in the United States of America

5 6 7 8 9 PM 06 05

ABOUT THIS BOOK

The book is written for supervisors, managers, or those who oversee a customer-service operation. That is, if you are responsible for a group of people, no matter how many or few, this book is for you.

The hard truth is that quality in customer-service interaction doesn't just happen. Unfortunately, we cannot hire people to fill customer-service jobs, tell them what to do, and then cross our fingers and pray that everything will be all right. Quality customer-service just doesn't work that way.

The premise of this book is threefold: (1) using specialized techniques, we can manage quality in a service operation just as we can in other enterprises that produce a more tangible product, (2) to achieve quality in the delivery of customer service, a specific set of management strategies must be followed, and (3) what managers do in this area has more influence over the quality of customer service than any other single factor.

Delivering quality customer-service requires knowledge, forethought and a great deal of concentrated effort doing, "the right things." This book outlines what these "right things" are and helps you to attain them.

I have attempted to present a straightforward, step-by-step process of what it takes to successfully manage a customer-service operation. THIS BOOK WILL HELP YOU SUCCEED. It has been designed to be interactive as well as informative. I would also hope that it is enjoyable as well as instructive.

William B. Martin
Claremont, California

CONTENTS

HOW THIS BOOK IS ORGANIZED
DEVELOPING A CUSTOMER-SERVICE PERSPECTIVE

STAGE I: UNDERSTAND YOUR CUSTOMERS 1
    What Is Your Specific Service Niche? 4
    What Are the Characteristics of the Services You Provide? 7
    Developing Your Customer Profile 9
    How Do Your Customers See You? 12
    Review and Action Plan 14

STAGE II: SET QUALITY SERVICE STANDARDS 17
    The Importance of Setting Quality Service Standards 19
    The Two Dimensions of Quality Service 20
    Writing Quality Service Standard Statements 25
    Prioritizing Your Quality Customer-Service Standards 29
    Review and Action Plan 31

STAGE III: BUILD A WINNING TEAM 33
    Putting Quality into the Design of Customer Jobs 35
    Writing Job Specs in Quality Customer-Service Terms 37
    Screening Job Applicants for Quality Customer-Service Abilities 39
    Training for Quality Customer-Service 41
    Quality Customer-Service Leadership 44
    A Supportive Organizational Climate 52
    Review and Action Plan 54

STAGE IV: CHECK UP REGULARLY 56
    A Service Audit System 59
    A Customer Feedback System 63
    Employee Feedback System 68
    Review and Action Plan 77

STAGE V: PROVIDE PROACTIVE PROBLEM SOLVING 79
    Create A Supportive Climate for Solving Customer-Service Problems . . 81
    Use Your Customer-Service Team to Identify Customer-Service
        Problem Areas 83
    Use Your Customer-Service Team as a Resource for Improving
        Service 87
    Turn Customer Problems into Opportunities for Better
        Customer-Service 89
    Review and Action Plan 91

ADDITIONAL CUSTOMER-SERVICE RESOURCES 94

HOW THIS BOOK IS ORGANIZED

This book is divided into five major sections. Each section represents one of the five stages in the customer-service management cycle. Individual sections are intended not only to enhance your understanding of that particular stage, but also to facilitate actual implementation of the principles and concepts introduced in the customer-service management cycle. You will be guided through the cycle as illustrated in the diagram below. This graphic will be repeated throughout the book to reinforce where you are in the customer-service cycle.

THE CUSTOMER SERVICE
MANAGEMENT CYCLE

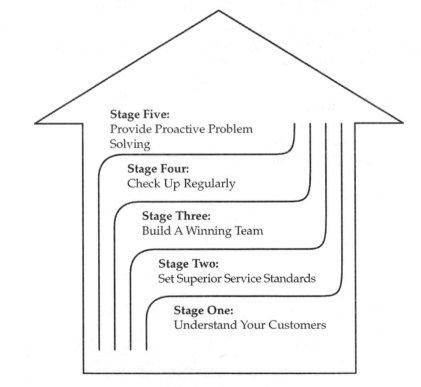

CUSTOMER SERVICE,
WHERE YOU WANT IT TO BE

Stage Five:
Provide Proactive Problem Solving

Stage Four:
Check Up Regularly

Stage Three:
Build A Winning Team

Stage Two:
Set Superior Service Standards

Stage One:
Understand Your Customers

CUSTOMER SERVICE,
WHERE IT IS NOW

A GUIDE FOR THE CHANGE AGENT

The customer-service management cycle begins with the level of customer service your organization currently provides. Properly <u>implemented</u> it <u>ultimately</u> <u>leads</u> to a new, <u>desired</u> level of service. In short, the cycle will take your organization from where it is now, to where you want it to be.

This book starts at Stage One and <u>proceeds</u> to Stage Five; however, in practice, the customer-service management cycle has no definite beginning or end. Rather, it represents a continuous process of improvement. Within the dynamics of organizational life, each stage of the customer-service management cycle has a profound effect on each of the other stages. As you will see, successful <u>implementation</u> of Stage Five will result in a better understanding of customers (Stage One), in addition to solving customer problems (Stage Five). In other words, there is a full circle in the customer-service management cycle.

The customer-service management cycle represents the stages necessary to successfully bring about a positive change within your organization. This book is a practical step-by-step "change agent's" guide which will help improve customer-service delivery systems within your organization.

DEVELOPING A CUSTOMER-SERVICE PERSPECTIVE

THE PERSPECTIVE REQUIRED

This book is based on a "customer-service perspective." A customer-service perspective asks you to look at your organization and the service you provide in a unique way.

A customer-service perspective maintains that THE MOST IMPORTANT ACTIVITY IN WHICH AN ORGANIZATION ENGAGES IS INTERACTING WITH CUSTOMERS. This is IT. This is the core of customer service. This is the *sine qua non*. This is the place where organization meets customer. This is the point of SERVICE ENCOUNTER. This is what Jan Carlzon of Scandinavian Airlines has succinctly labeled "THE MOMENT OF TRUTH."

WHEN THE CUSTOMER-SERVICE ENCOUNTER BECOMES THE MOMENT OF TRUTH FOR AN ORGANIZATION, THE ENTIRE FOCUS OF THAT ORGANIZATION IS LITERALLY TURNED UPSIDE DOWN.

Whether a high-paid, professional marking representative or an entry-level sales clerk makes the customer encounter, a customer-service perspective appreciates that every interaction has profound consequences on the success of the organization. This puts the power and authority of the organization at the level of customer contact. When this power and authority is truly respected and when the spotlight of the organization's priorities is focused securely on the point of customer contact, a customer-service perspective begins to emerge.

THE MANAGEMENT SKILLS REQUIRED

As a crucial function of the organization, customer contact systems need to be managed with the highest degree of enlightenment possible. Moreover, the management of service encounters does require a special set of knowledge and skills. In other words, MANAGING THE MOMENTS OF TRUTH SUCCESSFULLY REQUIRES THAT YOU AND YOUR ORGANIZATION NOT ONLY ASSUME A CUSTOMER-SERVICE PERSPECTIVE, BUT ALSO MANAGE IN A CERTAIN WAY. That is what this book is all about.

> "When the moments of truth go unmanaged, the quality of service regresses to mediocrity."
> Karl Albrecht/Ron Zemke
> *Service America*

TWO VIEWS OF ORGANIZATION

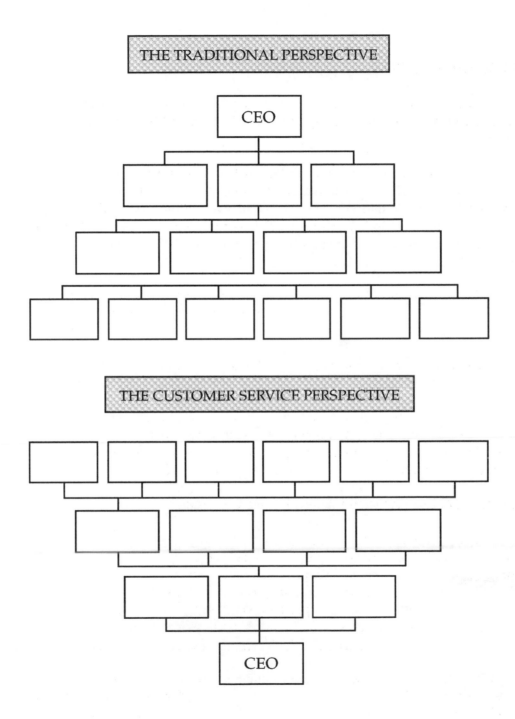

Stage I

UNDERSTAND YOUR CUSTOMERS

**CUSTOMER SERVICE,
WHERE YOU WANT IT TO BE**

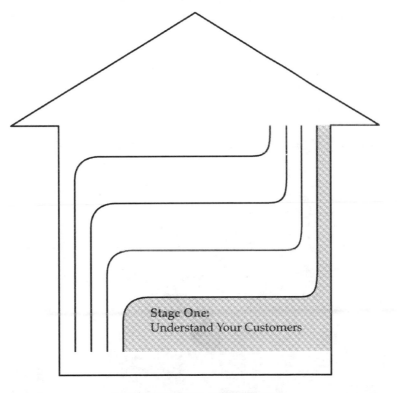

Stage One:
Understand Your Customers

**CUSTOMER SERVICE,
WHERE IT IS NOW**

UNDERSTAND YOUR CUSTOMERS

Stage One, UNDERSTAND YOUR CUSTOMERS, serves as a point of reference for the remaining four stages in the quality customer-service management cycle. This stage helps you define specifically the service you provide. It also will teach you how to become better acquainted with your customers.

The premise of this stage is—

> YOU CANNOT MANAGE A QUALITY CUSTOMER-SERVICE OPERA-TION UNLESS YOU UNDERSTAND THE NATURE OF WHAT IT IS YOU ARE PROVIDING, FULLY REALIZE WHAT YOUR CUSTOMERS WANT FROM YOU, AND HOW THEY PERCEIVE YOU FROM THE START.

"THESE ARE OUR CUSTOMERS, MS. STEVENS; IT'S OUR JOB TO UNDERSTAND THEM."

STAGE ONE ADDRESSES FOUR FUNDAMENTAL QUESTIONS:

1. WHAT IS YOUR *SPECIFIC* SERVICE <u>NICHE?</u>

2. WHAT ARE THE CHARACTERISTICS OF THE SERVICE(S) YOU PROVIDE?

3. WHO ARE YOUR CUSTOMERS AND WHAT DO THEY WANT?

4. HOW DO YOUR CUSTOMERS SEE YOU?

Developing some answers to these four questions will allow you to focus your customer-service <u>efforts</u> in the right direction—toward the customer.

"The purpose of business is to create and keep a customer."

Peter Drucker

WHAT IS YOUR SPECIFIC SERVICE NICHE?

THE SERVICE NICHE INVENTORY

The organization in which you work, whether it is a business enterprise, public agency or volunteer organization, operates within a given industry or domain. This is often referred to as a "market" or sometimes a "clientele."

Some organizations have a more focused view of what they are about than others. Some operate within a broad spectrum of customers, while others serve an extremely specialized market. Understanding the nature of your market is critical to organizational success. This is particularly true when it comes to delivering quality customer service. *THE ABILITY TO FOCUS YOUR EFFORTS IS CRUCIAL TO YOUR ABILITY TO PROVIDE QUALITY CUSTOMER SERVICE.*

That is why it is important to fully understand the segment, or niche, of the industry in which you serve.

YOUR SERVICE NICHE

This area of focus is your *SERVICE NICHE*. Your service niche is determined by two factors:

1) *THE SPECIFIC SERVICES* which you provide, and

2) *YOUR TARGETED CUSTOMERS.*

The services offered by your organization are, perhaps, a segment of all the services that make up the total industry. The *specific services* that you and your service team provide, in turn, may represent only a *portion* of all the services provided by your organization as a whole.

In like manner, the *specific targeted customers* for which you and your service team are responsible may represent only a part of your organization's total customer base, which, in turn, may be a segment of the totality of the market within your industry.

DETERMINE YOUR SERVICE NICHE

This page will help you focus on the nature of the service niche that you serve by summarizing your targeted services.

TARGETED SERVICES

1. What is the general industry within which your organization operates?

_____

2. The segment of the industry which comprises your organization's activities may be BROAD or NARROW in scope. If your organization focuses its attention on a specific set of services, or SEGMENT of those offered by the total industry, describe that segment here.

_____

_____

3. If the service for which YOU AND YOUR SERVICE TEAM are responsible is even more limited, describe these services below.

_____

_____

WHAT YOU HAVE OUTLINED AS YOUR *TARGETED SERVICES* AND YOUR *TARGETED CUSTOMERS* CONSTITUTE A DESCRIPTION OF YOUR *SERVICE NICHE.*

DETERMINE YOUR SERVICE NICHE (Continued)

This page will help you focus on the customers you serve.

TARGETED CUSTOMERS

The second part of defining your specific service niche is to identify your targeted customer base.

As with your service niche, your targeted customer base may range from broad to narrow.

Note: Unlike describing the service you provide, customers may be individuals or organizations or parts of organizations.

Here are a few categories commonly used to describe targeted customers:

INDIVIDUALS	ORGANIZATION
Size/Numbers	Size/Numbers
Income Level	Sales Level
Location	Location
Interests	Industry/Function

1. How would you describe the customer base for your industry, as a whole?

   _____

2. How would you describe your organization's targeted customer base? (Use the categories listed above, if helpful.)

   _____

   _____

3. Using the categories above, describe the targeted customers to whom you and your service team are directly responsible.

   _____

   _____

WHAT YOU CAN DO AS A MANAGER TO PROVIDE QUALITY CUSTOMER SERVICE TO THIS NICHE SHOULD BE YOUR FOCUS FOR THE REMAINDER OF THIS BOOK.

WHAT ARE THE CHARACTERISTICS OF THE SERVICES YOU PROVIDE?

Understanding your SERVICE CHARACTERISTICS will allow you to appreciate how the services you provide are SEEN BY YOUR CUSTOMERS.

CONSIDER THESE TEN SERVICE CHARACTERISTICS:

1. **People/Things Orientation.**
   Is the service you provide more people oriented or is it more oriented toward things (i.e., machines, equipment, and technology)?

2. **High Tech/Low Tech.**
   If technology is involved in the delivery of the service provided, is it state-of-the-art, or are more traditional tools and/or systems used.

3. **Personal Interaction.**
   The characteristic can be divided into three parts.
   Physical: Do the parties involved in the service have to see each other? How close are they to each other? What type of touching is involved?
   Mental: To what extent does the interaction demand the people involved to think, to analyze, to comprehend?
   Emotional: To what extent does the interaction rely on emotional-based-reactions and/or situations?

4. **Time Involvement.**
   How long (in duration) does the service take? How *frequently* does it occur?

5. **Location.**
   Does the service take place at the customer's site, your locale, or somewhere else?

6. **Complexity.**
   Actual: How complex is the service provided? How complicated are delivery systems?
   Visual: How much complexity does the customer see? Do service delivery systems *appear* to be simple when they are really not?

7. **Accommodation.**
   How flexible and adaptable are the service systems? To what extent can they be adjusted to meet unique or different customer needs or requests?

8. **Numbers Served Per Transaction.**
   How many customers are provided service during a single service transaction? One or two? A small group? Hundreds? Thousands?

9. **Training.**
   How much training, education, and/or expertise is needed to deliver service?

10. **Supervision.**
    How much supervision does the service system require?

DEVELOP A SERVICE PROFILE

DEVELOP A SERVICE PROFILE

YOUR SERVICE PROFILE

CIRCLE THE RESPONSE THAT MOST CLOSELY MATCHES THE
NATURE OF THE SERVICE YOUR SERVICE TEAM PROVIDES.

1. People/Things Orientation	More Things	More People
2. Level of Technology	Hi Tech	Lo Tech
3. Personal Interaction: Physical	Hi	Lo
Mental	Hi	Lo
Emotional	Hi	Lo
4. Time Involvement: Duration	Long	Short
Frequency	Hi	Lo
5. Location	Their Place	Our Place
6. Complexity: Actual	Hi	Lo
Visual	Hi	Lo
7. Accommodation Ability	Hi	Lo
8. Numbers Served Per Transaction	One	Many
9. Training Required	Much	Little
10. Supervision Needed	Much	Little

DEVELOPING YOUR CUSTOMER PROFILE

On page 6 you described your customer within your service niche. *CAN THIS GROUP OF CUSTOMERS BE DIVIDED INTO SMALLER MORE HOMOGE-NEOUS GROUPS?*

If so, each of these groupings represents a *SEGMENT* of your total group of customers.

YOUR PROFILES FOR EACH CUSTOMER SEGMENT MAY DIFFER. Up to three different customer segments can be profiled using the form on page 10.

Fill in the appropriate information on the next two pages as completely as possible. If you don't know some of the information asked for, make an effort to find out. The more you know about your customers, the more you are able to offer the service that meets their needs.

Note: There are two profiles: one for customers as individuals and one for customers as organizations. Fill out the one(s) appropriate to your customer base.

> *HERE ARE SOME DEFINITIONS THAT MAY BE HELPFUL IN CREATING A PROFILE OF YOUR CUSTOMERS.*

Values and Beliefs
Values and beliefs reflect the central core of what's important to your customers. What is their code? What is good? What is held sacred?

Attitudes
Attitudes are ways of looking at things. Common held attitudes reflect ways of looking at life, work, marriage, commitment, doing business, etc.

Social Habits and Norms
Social habits and norms are commonly agreed-upon acceptable behaviors. How do people behave? What do they do? What is the "right" and "wrong" way of doing something?

Preferences
Preferences are what your customer likes. What *do* your customers like? When offered a choice what do they choose?

Expectations
What do your customers hope to get from you? What do they want? When they do business with you, what are their bottom line expectations?

DEVELOPING CUSTOMER PROFILE (Continued)

CUSTOMER PROFILE (INDIVIDUALS)

	Segment #1	Segment #2	Segment #3
Demographic Charcteristics			
Age	_____	_____	_____
Gender	_____	_____	_____
Education level	_____	_____	_____
Income	_____	_____	_____
Family Size	_____	_____	_____
Type of housing	_____	_____	_____

Psychographic Characteristics

Values/Beliefs
_____
_____
_____

Attitudes
_____
_____

Social Habits
_____
_____

Preferences
_____
_____

Expectations
_____
_____
_____

DEVELOPING CUSTOMER PROFILE
(Continued)

CUSTOMER PROFILE (ORGANIZATIONS)

	Segment #1	Segment #2	Segment #3
Demographic Characteristics			
Industry	_____	_____	_____
Size	_____	_____	_____
Locations	_____	_____	_____

Organization Culture Characteristics

Values/Beliefs _____

_____

_____

Attitudes _____

_____

_____

Norms/Social Habits _____

_____

Preferences _____

_____

_____

Expectations _____

_____

_____

HOW DO YOUR CUSTOMERS SEE YOU?

YOUR SERVICE SILHOUETTE

Your *SERVICE SILHOUETTE* is how your customers perceive you from the start. Service silhouettes are formed by the customer BEFORE they make use of your services. They emerge BEFORE a clearer service image develops out of your customer-service interaction.

HOW CUSTOMERS SEE YOU IS AFFECTED BY

–your *SERVICE CHARACTERISTICS*
–their *WANTS AND NEEDS*

PLUS

–their *PERCEPTION OF THE FOLLOWING SERVICE SILHOUETTE DETERMINERS.*

The Purpose of Your Service
Do your customers want a task or function completed? Is their purpose for using your service entirely for enjoyment or entertainment. Or are both task and entertainment involved?

The Degree of Necessity
How necessary is your service to customers? Can they get along without it? How badly is it needed?

The Magnitude of Importance
How important is the service to your customers? How badly is it wanted?

View of Results
Are the results of the service viewed in a positive way? Do they make a positive contribution in the customer's mind? Or, are results perceived in a negative way—as reducing something undesirable?

Relative Costs
How expensive is your service? From the customer's point of view, does it require a major commitment of money?

Perceived Risks
What does the customer stand to lose by accepting your service? In the customer's mind are the risks major or minor?

NOTE: THE IMPORTANCE OF EACH OF THESE FACTORS MAY VARY AMONG CUSTOMERS AND CUSTOMER SEGMENTS.

ASSESSING YOUR SERVICE SILHOUETTE DETERMINERS

Since the perception of factors may vary from customer-to-customer or from segment-to-segment, when responding to the assessment below, think of the "typical" or "average" customer for up to three customer segments.

HOW DO YOUR CUSTOMERS SEE YOU?	Segment #1	Segment #2	Segment #3
1. How do they see the PURPOSE of the service? Pleasure Task	_____	_____	_____
2. How NECESSARY is it? Necessity Choice	_____	_____	_____
3. How IMPORTANT is it? Important Unimportant	_____	_____	_____
4. How are RESULTS viewed? Positive Negative Contribution Reduction	_____	_____	_____
5. What is the perceived COST? High Med Low	_____	_____	_____
6. What are the perceived RISKS? High Med Low	_____	_____	_____

REVIEW OF STAGE I

Delivering quality customer service starts with knowing as much about your customers as possible. In the first important stage, we have presented four fundamental steps to help you understand your customers better.

1) KNOW YOUR SERVICE NICHE
   by focusing–

   on the specific services you provide your targeted customers within the larger organization and industry setting.

2) NOTE YOUR SERVICE CHARACTERISTICS
   by assessing–

people/things	complexity
high tech/low tech	accommodation
personal interaction	number served
time involvement	training required
location	supervision needed

3) REALIZE WHO YOUR CUSTOMERS ARE AND WHAT THEY WANT
   by knowing their–

   demographics
   psychographics
   organizational cultures

4) APPRECIATE YOUR SERVICE SILHOUETTE
   by assessing how customers see your service's–

purpose	results
necessity	costs
importance	risks

YOUR ACTION PLAN FOR STAGE ONE

After reviewing the four approaches presented in Stage One, to help you develop a better understanding of your customers, what are YOU going to do NOW to cultivate a broader awareness of the customers you and your service team serve? Write a brief action plan in the space provided below:

STAGE II

SET QUALITY SERVICE STANDARDS

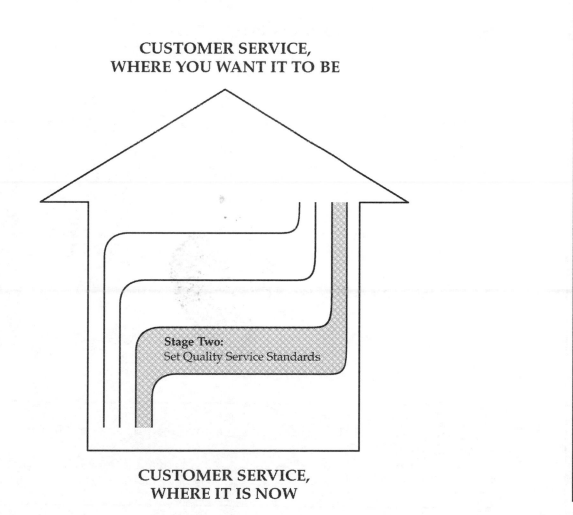

**CUSTOMER SERVICE,
WHERE YOU WANT IT TO BE**

Stage Two:
Set Quality Service Standards

**CUSTOMER SERVICE,
WHERE IT IS NOW**

SET QUALITY SERVICE STANDARDS

In Stage Two of the Customer-Service Management Process, you begin to transform your service silhouette, as seen by your customers, into a well-focused, sharp SERVICE IMAGE.

THE FIRST STEP IN DOING THIS IS TO SET–

CLEAR,

CONCISE,

OBSERVABLE, AND

REALISTIC

SERVICE STANDARDS

> "Quality is dependable when you have an agreed-upon standard of measurement."
>
> Diane Bone/Rick Griggs
> *Quality at Work*

THE IMPORTANCE OF SETTING QUALITY SERVICE STANDARDS

1. ESTABLISH A TARGET: Written service standards establish a goal—a target—toward which all people on your service team can direct their efforts. It gives them a clear sense of what to strive for and how high to reach. It establishes a sense of purpose, direction for them. It keeps them focused, on target, headed in the right direction.

2. COMMUNICATE EXPECTATIONS: Clear, concise, observable and realistic service standards form a common base of expectations for all service behavior. By establishing them you are communicating to all your people, "This is what we all expect. This is what all of us want. This is what an excellent job is all about." When you do this you have communicated your expectations loud and clear to everybody involved in customer service. Everybody is on the same wavelength. What you want is common knowledge. There are no surprises about what is expected.

3. CREATE A VALUABLE MANAGEMENT TOOL: Once you have developed a complete list of service standards, they can become part of recruiting profiles, job descriptions, and hiring decisions. Your standards can also easily carry over into your training efforts, so your service operational standards become part and parcel of the standards toward which all employees are prepared for their jobs. In addition, your clear, concise, observable, and realistic standards can become the foundation of a meaningful and productive employee performance appraisal system, a system that evaluates the behaviors important to customer service at the level of excellence accepted by everybody in your team.

BY ESTABLISHING CLEAR, CONCISE, OBSERVABLE, AND REALISTIC STANDARDS YOU ARE DEFINING WHAT YOU WANT YOUR SERVICE IMAGE TO BE.

THIS IS WHERE QUALITY CUSTOMER SERVICE BEGINS!

THE TWO DIMENSIONS OF QUALITY SERVICE

Quality customer service consists of two integral dimensions.

1. THE PROCEDURAL DIMENSION

This dimension of service is systematic in nature. It deals with service delivery systems. It encompasses the procedures of how things get done. It provides the mechanisms by which customers' needs are met. This side of service is *THE PROCEDURAL DIMENSION OF CUSTOMER SERVICE.*

2. THE PERSONAL DIMENSION

While the procedural dimension is cool, rational, and systematic, the other dimension of customer service is warm, often irrational, and certainly unpredictable. This is the human side of service. It is interpersonal in nature, and it encompasses the attitudes, behaviors, and verbal skills that are present in every personal service interaction. This side of service is *THE PERSONAL DIMENSION OF CUSTOMER SERVICE.*

YOUR LIST OF QUALITY SERVICE STANDARDS MUST INCORPORATE BOTH THE PROCEDURAL AND PERSONAL SERVICE DIMENSIONS.

To help you and your service team generate your own list of service standards, seven critical areas in both the procedural dimension and the personal dimension are outlined on pages 21 and 23. These are vital areas of customer service that a complete list of service standards should address. Each of the fourteen areas are offered to help you develop your own clear, concise, observable, and realistic customer-service standards.

> "In service-encounter management, the components for success might be stated as details, details, details."
>
> G. Lynn Shostack
> "Planning the Service Encounter"
> *The Service Encounter*

SEVEN STANDARD AREAS IN THE PROCEDURAL DIMENSION OF QUALITY SERVICE

Check the box that applies to your organization.

1. **TIMING**. What are your timing standards for delivering service to customers? How long should it take? Are there several steps that require different timing standards? Does timeliness equate to promptness? Or can service at times be too fast, causing the customer to feel rushed?

❏ We have timing standards.

❏ We need new or revised timing standards.

2. **FLOW**. How do the various components of the service delivery system coordinate, cooperating, and/or mesh with each other? How do you control the flow of goods or service to the customer? How can you avoid back-ups and log jams? What are the indicators of this that can be seen or measured?

❏ We have procedures in place to accommodate a smooth work flow.

❏ We need help in this area.

3. **ACCOMMODATION**. How flexible are your systems? Can this flexibility be adapted to varying customer needs and/or requests? How convenient are they for customers? How do they make the customers' service experience easier? Are your service systems designed around your customers' needs? What are your observable indicators of accommodating systems?

❏ We are flexible when it comes to customer needs.

❏ Our systems come first, our customers' second.

4. **ANTICIPATION**. How well can you anticipate customer needs? How can you be one step ahead of customers so service can be provided without them having to remind you service is needed? How do you know what will happen? How do you know when you and your team have anticipated correctly? What indicators of proper anticipation by your service delivery systems can be seen or measured?

❏ We normally keep one step ahead of our customers.

❏ We never seem to stay ahead of our customers' needs.

SEVEN PROCEDURAL STANDARDS
(Continued)

5. **COMMUNICATION**. Service delivery systems cannot function optimally without effective and efficient communication within the system and between you and your customers. How do you know when messages are communicated thoroughly, accurately, and in a timely way? What are the signs of effective communication? How do you know when communication has broken down? Is it too late? What measurable standards reflect effective communication in your operation?

- ❏ Our communication is A-O.K.

- ❏ We need help with our communication systems.

6. **CUSTOMER FEEDBACK.** How do you find out what your customers are thinking? How are customer feedback systems used to improve service? How do you know if your customers are pleased, displeased, satisfied, dissatisfied, happy, or unhappy? What are your observable indicators of effective customer feedback systems? How do you know when they are working correctly?

- ❏ We encourage customer feedback and routinely collect and analyze it.

- ❏ Feedback is not a priority with us.

7. **ORGANIZATION AND SUPERVISION.** Efficient procedural service requires organization, and organization, in turn, requires supervision. Who does what in your service operation? How are you organized? What would your optimal organizational structure look like? How should it be supervised? What role should the supervisor take in the service delivery process? How are all the parts of the service delivery system kept coordinated with each other? What are the signs that can be seen or measured that tell you all is going well?

- ❏ We have a clear and efficient organization.

- ❏ We lack organization when it comes to customers.

ANSWERING THESE QUESTIONS WILL HELP YOU AND YOUR TEAM DEVELOP CLEAR, CONCISE, OBSERVABLE, AND REALISTIC SERVICE STANDARDS.

SEVEN STANDARDS AREAS IN THE PERSONAL DIMENSION OF QUALITY SERVICE

Check the statement that best describes your organization.

1. **APPEARANCE**. A customer's positive or negative reaction to a given customer-service interaction is strongly influenced by what he or she sees. Sight is a dominant sense that colors the perceptions of our experiences. What do you want your customers to see when they approach or are approached by one of your service persons? How do you want the service person to appear? What mood, atmosphere, or image should your service person reflect? What are the observable signs that appearance standards are being met?

 We have guidelines that we follow.

 Appearance is not a big issue with us.

2. **ATTITUDE: BODY LANGUAGE & TONE OF VOICE**. Since we can't see the attitude of service personnel directly, we see it through their body language and tone of voice. Our attitude shows for all to see. Our body language and tone of voice conveys the "real" message being communicated. How do members of your service team convey proper service attitudes through their body language? How about smile, eye contact, posture as well as hand and body movements? How would you describe the ideally desired body language for the service you provide? How would you describe the ideal tone of voice you want your service team to convey? How do you know when these are being conveyed? What are your observable indicators?

❑ We are famous for our positive attitude.

❑ Attitude is not important.

3. **ATTENTIVENESS**. Attentiveness involves tuning in to customers' unique needs and wants. It is being sensitive. It is treating each and every customer in a special, unique way that recognizes his or her individuality. In what ways can your service personnel be attentive? How can they make customers feel special? What different customer groups require varying sensitivities? What can your service people do to address these unique needs?

❑ We stress attentiveness to customers' wants and needs.

 We treat everyone exactly the same.

SEVEN PERSONAL STANDARDS
(Continued)

4. **TACT**. Tact involves not only how messages are sent but also the choice of words. Certain language can turn customers off and, therefore, should be avoided. What is the right thing to say under differing circumstances? What should always be said during a customer interaction? How should customers be addressed? How often and when should customers be called by their name?

- ❏ Tact is essential to our success.
- ❏ Forget tact, we just do our job!

5. **GUIDANCE**. How can service personnel be of help to customers? How should they guide decisions, give advice, offer suggestions? What resources should be available to assist in helping the customer? What level of knowledge is required on the service person's part before proper guidance can be given? How do you know when the knowledge level is up to standard? How can this standard be measured?

- ❏ Customers rely on our assistance.
- ❏ Much of the time, we know less than our customers.

6. **SELLING SKILLS.** Selling is an integral part of service whether it is selling products or selling service. The function of service is to cultivate, facilitate, and accumulate sales. Therefore, to what extent are selling skills valued among the service staff? What constitutes effective selling skills for the service you provide? What are the observable, or measurable, indicators of effective selling? What are your selling standards?

- ❏ Everyone in our organization is a sales person.
- ❏ Selling is strictly for marketing types.

7. **GRACIOUS PROBLEM SOLVING.** How should customer complaints be handled? How can upset customers be made happy? How should difficult and rude customers be dealt with? Is the customer always right? If so, how far can you go in maintaining that standard? Who should handle customer complaints and problems? What is their realm of authority? How do you know when problems are handled graciously? What are the indicators and how can they be seen or measured?

- ❏ We pride ourselves on problem solving.
- ❏ Problems? We don't have problems.

> "All contacts with an organization are a critical part of our perceptions and judgments about that organization. The quality of the *people contacts*, however, are often the firmest and most lasting."   Karl Albrecht/Ron Zemke
> *Service America*

WRITING QUALITY SERVICE STANDARD STATEMENTS

The purpose of this exercise is to help you and your service team WRITE quality customer-service standards. *Quality service standards are always clear, concise, observable, and realistic.*

Below, a few sample *QUALITY SERVICE STANDARDS* are compared with a few samples of weak service standards. (These examples were borrowed from two different restaurants.)

WEAK SERVICE STANDARDS	QUALITY SERVICE STANDARDS:
Timeliness: Upon entering the service area, customers are greeted quickly.	Timeliness: Upon entering the service area, customers are greeted within 30 seconds.
Anticipation: Service employees think at least one step ahead of customers.	Anticipation: Customers receive water refills without having to ask.
Attitude: Employees are friendly to customers.	Attitude: The hostess talks with the customers while showing them to their seats.
Customer Feedback: Customers are listened to.	Customer Feedback: The manager on duty personally deals with every customer complaint directly with the customer.
Appearance: Employees look neat, clean and ready for work.	Appearance: Employees are attired exactly as specified in the dress code described in the Employee Handbook.

WHAT DO THE QUALITY SERVICE STANDARDS HAVE IN COMMON?

NOTE: WHILE THE WEAK SERVICE STANDARDS ARE TOO GENERAL AND VAGUE TO BE OF ANY VALUE, THE QUALITY SERVICE STANDARDS ARE—
- CLEAR...They are precise in meaning.
- CONCISE...They are short and to the point.
- OBSERVABLE...They can be seen or measured.
- REALISTIC...They are practical and obtainable.

WRITE YOUR OWN QUALITY SERVICE STANDARDS

TRY WRITING A FEW CLEAR, CONCISE, OBSERVABLE, AND REALISTIC SERVICE STANDARDS FOR YOUR SERVICE OPERATION. Note: The purpose of this exercise is to give you some practice writing quality service standards. The creation of a complete listing of service standards requires a committed team of people consisting of a cross-section of your customer-service employees working together. GENERATION OF SERVICE STANDARDS FOR YOUR TEAM SHOULD BE A TEAM EFFORT, NOT A ONE-PERSON JOB.

TIMELINESS, standard statement: _____

_____

_____

FLOW, standard statement: _____

_____

_____

ACCOMMODATION, standard statement: _____

_____

_____

ANTICIPATION, standard statement: _____

_____

_____

COMMUNICATION, standard statement: _____

_____

_____

CUSTOMER FEEDBACK, standard statement: _____

_____

_____

ORGANIZATION AND SUPERVISION, standard statement: _____

_____

_____

APPEARANCE, standard statement: _____

_____

_____

ATTITUDE: BODY LANGUAGE & TONE OF VOICE, standard statement: ____

_____

_____

ATTENTIVENESS, standard statement: _____

_____

_____

TACT, standard statement: _____

_____

_____

GUIDANCE, standard statement: _____

_____

_____

SELLING SKILLS, standard statement: _____

_____

_____

GRACIOUS PROBLEM SOLVING, standard statement:_____

_____

_____

GUIDELINES FOR DEVELOPING QUALITY SERVICE STANDARDS

A complete set of guidelines for writing performance standards is presented in the Crisp Publication *Quality at Work* by Diane Bone and Rick Griggs. Here are a number of guidelines adapted from that book that you should keep in mind when creating quality customer-service standards.

1. Standards should be planned and agreed upon by all affected employees, including customers when possible.

2. They should come as close to zero defects as is humanly possible for your service.

3. They should be stated clearly and completely in writing.

4. They must satisfy your customer's requirements.

5. They must be workable and understandable.

6. They must be supported by upper management (or they won't work).

7. Deviation from the standard must not be accepted once the standards are established.

8. If the standard is not working or becomes outdated, it should be changed.

9. New standards should be added as needed. All affected employees must agree and sign off on the new standard.

10. They must reflect organizational goals.

11. They should be created and met with care.

12. They must be communicated effectively and continually.

PRIORITIZING YOUR QUALITY CUSTOMER-SERVICE STANDARDS

The nature of the service that you render will influence which of the service standards ARE MORE IMPORTANT THAN OTHERS. All standards may not be created equally. Here are three examples that explain why.

Situation A

If your service is rendered ENTIRELY BY MACHINE OR THROUGH THE MAIL, the personal dimension of service may have little or no bearing on the quality of service that you provide the customer.

Situation B

If your service is performed ENTIRELY OVER THE TELEPHONE, some service standards i.e., appearance, may take secondary importance to other procedural and personal dimension standards.

Situation C

If your service involves DIRECT PERSONAL CONTACT with customers, the relative importance of personal dimension standards to procedural dimension standards may vary with the nature of your service. For example, whether you and your service team actually *perform* the service or *represent* the service that is rendered at a later date, may make a difference in how you prioritize your customer-service standards.

COMPLETE THE EXERCISE ON THE FOLLOWING PAGE TO GAIN AN APPRECIATION OF WHICH SERVICE STANDARDS ARE OF UPMOST IMPORTANCE *IN YOUR SPECIFIC OPERATION.*

PRIORITIZING YOUR SERVICE STANDARDS: AN EXERCISE

With your *specific* service operation in mind—

(1) Determine the relative importance of procedural standards to personal standards by expressing it in a ratio.

(for example): 20% procedural   80% personal
90% procedural   10% personal
50% procedural   50% personal

(2) Next, rank *separately* the standards in each dimension. Give the most important standard, in a given dimension, a "1" and the next most important standard a "2" and so forth. Rank one dimension and then rank the other.

I. MY PROCEDURAL-TO-PERSONAL-DIMENSION-RATIO OF IMPORTANCE IS:

_____% PROCEDURAL   _____% PERSONAL

II. My rankings of the standard areas within each dimension are:

PROCEDURAL DIMENSION	PERSONAL DIMENSION
___ Accommodation	___ Appearance
___ Anticipation	___ Attitude; body language, tone of voice
___ Timeliness	___ Attentiveness
___ Flow	___ Tact
___ Communication	___ Guidance
___ Customer Feedback	___ Selling Skills
___ Organization/Supervision	___ Gracious Problem Solving

REVIEW OF STAGE II

A. You must establish quality service standards for (1) service systems represented by the procedural dimension of service and (2) personal customer contact reflected in the personal dimension of service.

B. Seven areas in which you should consider establishing procedural service standards include:

- timing
- flow
- accommodation
- communication
- customer feedback
- organization and supervision

C. Seven areas in which you should consider establishing personal service standards include:

- appearance
- attitude: body language & tone of voice
- attentiveness
- tact
- guidance
- selling skills
- gracious problem solving

D. Written quality service standards should be:

- clear
- concise
- observable
- realistic

E. The nature of your service operation will determine the priority you place on each of the fourteen service standard areas.

F. The establishment of quality service standards needs to be a TOTAL TEAM EFFORT.

YOUR ACTION PLAN FOR STAGE II

After reviewing what it takes to develop quality service standards, what are YOU going to do NOW to make them a reality in your customer-service operation? Write a brief ACTION PLAN in the space below.

> Setting quality service standards not only will help you establish precise targets to aim for and assist you in communicating your expectations clearly to your service team, they will also serve you well when implementing the next three stages of the customer-service management process.

STAGE III

BUILD A WINNING TEAM

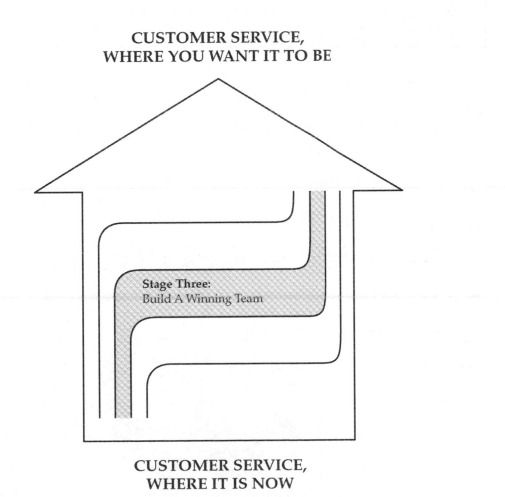

**CUSTOMER SERVICE,
WHERE YOU WANT IT TO BE**

Stage Three:
Build A Winning Team

**CUSTOMER SERVICE,
WHERE IT IS NOW**

BUILD A WINNING CUSTOMER-SERVICE TEAM

All the work you have completed in generating clear, concise, observable and reasonable quality customer-service standards will have little impact on your organization and your service image UNLESS YOU PUT THEM TO WORK FOR YOU.

YOU CAN PUT YOUR SERVICE STANDARDS TO WORK FOR YOU BY BUILDING A WINNING CUSTOMER-SERVICE TEAM.

STAGE THREE PROVIDES SIX STEPS TO DO JUST THAT. EACH STEP WILL BE COVERED IN THE NEXT SEVERAL PAGES OF THIS SECTION.

HOW TO BUILD A WINNING CUSTOMER-SERVICE TEAM:

STEP ONE: DESIGN QUALITY CUSTOMER-SERVICE JOBS

STEP TWO: WRITE JOB SPECIFICATIONS IN QUALITY CUSTOMER-SERVICE TERMS

STEP THREE: SCREEN JOB APPLICANTS FOR QUALITY CUSTOMER-SERVICE ABILITIES

STEP FOUR: TRAIN FOR QUALITY CUSTOMER-SERVICE SKILLS

STEP FIVE: PRACTICE QUALITY LEADERSHIP SKILLS

STEP SIX: ENCOURAGE A SUPPORTIVE ORGANIZATIONAL CLIMATE

STEP 1

BUILD A WINNING TEAM BY PUTTING QUALITY INTO THE DESIGN OF CUSTOMER JOBS

DESIGNING QUALITY CUSTOMER-SERVICE JOBS

You can design quality into your customer-service jobs by:

1. STATING THE PURPOSE OF THE JOB
   - What is the ultimate service desired?
   - What is the desired end result of the service?

2. EXPLAINING WHAT THE PERSON ACTUALLY *DOES* IN THIS JOB
   - What are the most important duties?
   - What are the secondary duties?
   - How often are the duties performed?
   - What is the nature and scope of decision making?

3. SPECIFYING *HOW* THE PERSON ACTUALLY PERFORMS THIS JOB
   - What methods, skills and/or technologies are used?
   - What are the general working conditions (i.e., place, hours, hazards, advantages, co-workers)?

4. STRESSING THE STANDARDS OF EXCELLENCE FOR THIS JOB
   - What procedural service standards apply to this job?
   - What personal service standards apply to this job?
   - How is a quality job measured?

5. DESCRIBING HOW THIS JOB RELATES TO OTHERS
   - What internal and external contacts are involved?
   - What are the reporting relationships?

YOUR JOB DESIGN MATRIX

Here is an opportunity for you to design QUALITY into a selected customer-service job by filling in the blanks.

JOB DESIGN STEPS   Job Title: _____

Purpose: _____

_____

_____

Duties: _____

_____

_____

Methods: _____

_____

_____

Standards: _____

_____

_____

Relations: _____

_____

_____

(This page may be copied without further permission from the publisher.)

STEP 2

BUILD A WINNING TEAM BY WRITING JOB SPECIFICATIONS IN QUALITY CUSTOMER-SERVICE TERMS

On pages 35 and 36 you had an opportunity to incorporate quality customer standards into the design of a selected customer-service job.

The next step is to describe *THE PERSON* needed to fill this job.

> Describing the *PEOPLE QUALIFICATIONS* required to fill a particular job is referred to as a *JOB SPECIFICATION* or *JOB SPEC*, for short.

HERE IS HOW YOU CAN INCORPORATE QUALITY CUSTOMER-SERVICE STANDARDS IN YOUR JOB SPECS.

1. LIST ALL THE CRITICAL KNOWLEDGE NEEDED TO PERFORM THE JOB
   - What does the person need to know about the job, its methods, the product, service, customers?
   - What educational level is desired/required?
   - What training is required, including customer-service training?

2. OUTLINE ALL THE VITAL SKILLS NEEDED TO PERFORM THIS JOB
   - What will the job holder have to do?
   - What task skills are involved?
   - What people skills are part of the job?

3. REVIEW OTHER BEHAVIOR ATTRIBUTES NEEDED
   - In addition to specific job skills, what other, more general, job related behaviors are necessary to perform this job at a quality level (e.g., problem-solving abilities, patience, assertiveness, etc.)?

4. SPECIFY SKILL STANDARDS
   - What is the defined level of excellence for task and people skills?
   - What are the observable or measurable indicators of these standards?

5. DESCRIBE THE RESULTS EXPECTED
   - What is the desired outcome of this job?
   - How will end-performance be measured?

YOUR JOB SPECIFICATION MATRIX

Describe below the person ideally qualified to fill your selected customer-service job by filling in the blanks.

JOB SPECIFICATIONS   Job Title: _____

Knowledge Needed: _____

_____

_____

Skills Needed: _____

_____

_____

Behavioral Attributes Needed: _____

_____

_____

Skill/Behavior Standards: _____

_____

_____

Expected Results: _____

_____

(This page may be copied without further permission from the publisher.)

STEP 3

BUILD A WINNING TEAM BY SCREEN-ING JOB APPLICANTS FOR QUALITY CUSTOMER-SERVICE ABILITIES

HOW TO GATHER QUALITY CUSTOMER-SERVICE RELATED DATA FROM JOB APPLICANTS

A job interview needs to determine how a candidate will function in every-day job activities. Methods to gather this information must be job—cus-tomer-service—centered and pursued without discrimination. Questions should stimulate the applicant to respond naturally. Ways in which this can be done include the following:

1. ASK GENERAL, OPEN ENDED QUESTIONS THAT DO NOT SUGGEST A PARTICULAR ANSWER. Here are a few examples.
   - What responsibilities of your last job did you like best?
   - What do you consider most important when working with customers?
   - Describe how you would handle an angry of difficult customer.
   - Describe what you have done and how you felt upon entering a room full of strangers.
   - What have you done in the past that reflects your enjoyment of other people?
   - What particularly funny thing has happened to you lately?
   - What job accomplishment do you feel particularly proud of?

2. LISTEN CAREFULLY TO EACH RESPONSE; THEN DECIDE ON YOUR NEXT QUESTION.
   A good interviewer spends nearly 80 PERCENT of the time LISTENING. Many inexperienced interviewers are in such a hurry to get to the next question, they fail to hear the applicant's response. Listen attentively to each answer. Often an answer will determine the next question. If the response does not provide enough information, say, "tell me more," or "can you be more specific?"

3. STIMULATE VALUE JUDGMENTS.
   Ask a candidate how he or she feels about difficult customers, personal commitment to working with customers, co-workers, etc.

4. PROBE "CHOICE POINTS."
   Choice points are situations that require the applicant to explain why they selected one course of action over another. For example, some choice points might be: why they selected a certain major in college, why they liked certain parts of previous jobs, why they feel they can do well in this job.

A PROFILE OF THE IDEAL CUSTOMER-SERVICE CANDIDATE

USE THIS PROFILE AS A CHECKLIST TO REFLECT A JOB CANDIDATE'S ANSWERS TO YOUR QUESTIONS.

Did the candidate reflect the following predictors of customer-service success in his or her responses to your questions?

YES NO

- ❏ ❏ A GENUINE LIKING OF PEOPLE

- ❏ ❏ AN ENJOYMENT OF WORKING FOR AND SERVING OTHERS

- ❏ ❏ A STRONG SOCIAL NEED

- ❏ ❏ AN ABILITY TO FEEL COMFORTABLE AMONG STRANGERS

- ❏ ❏ A SENSE OF BELONGING TO A GROUP OR PLACE

- ❏ ❏ AN ABILITY TO CONTROL FEELINGS

- ❏ ❏ A SENSITIVITY TOWARD PEOPLE AND ABILITY TO SHOW COMPASSION OR EMPATHY

- ❏ ❏ A SENSE OF BEING IN CONTROL OF YOUR LIFE AND WHAT HAPPENS TO YOU

- ❏ ❏ A GENERAL SENSE OF TRUSTING OTHERS

- ❏ ❏ A HIGH LEVEL OF SELF ESTEEM

- ❏ ❏ A TRACK RECORD OF COMPETENCE

TRY TO ASK QUESTIONS THAT GIVE THE CANDIDATE AN OPPORTUNITY TO REFLECT THESE CUSTOMER-SERVICE SUCCESS PREDICTORS.

The more items you check "yes" after a job interview, the higher degree of confidence you can have in this applicant's POTENTIAL to do well in a customer-service job.

NOTE: For assistance in asking the right kinds of questions during a job interview, you should refer to the Crisp Publication, *Quality Interviewing*, by Robert B. Maddux.

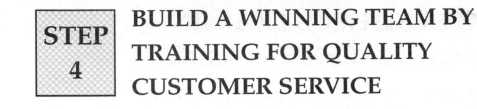

<table>
<tr><td>STEP
4</td><td># BUILD A WINNING TEAM BY TRAINING FOR QUALITY CUSTOMER SERVICE</td></tr>
</table>

Quality customer service will not happen unless you train for it to happen. Space in this book does not permit a complete discussion of how to design and deliver quality training programs, but what we can do is give you an opportunity to assess the training you now provide.

So with this in mind, please respond to the "Customer-Service Training Program Assessment Scale" on pages 42 and 43. Those items that receive low scores should be targeted for immediate improvement.

ASSESSMENT AHEAD →

CUSTOMER-SERVICE TRAINING PROGRAM ASSESSMENT SCALE

Rate your current customer-service training program according to the criteria for an excellent training program below. Circle your response for each item.

	Yes	Fairly Well	Some-what	Barely	No
1. The customer-service skills the trainee will be able to perform at the end of training are clearly delineated.	5	4	3	2	1
2. The knowledge the trainee should have about customer service at the end of the training program is clearly described.	5	4	3	2	1
3. The knowledge and skills learned about customer service in the training match those required of the job.	5	4	3	2	1
4. The customer-service training program is presented in an organized and systematic format.	5	4	3	2	1
5. The customer-service training is divided into a series of lessons or units.	5	4	3	2	1
6. Completion criteria for each learning unit are clear.	5	4	3	2	1
7. The program provides time for practicing customer-service skills away from the job, itself.	5	4	3	2	1
8. The trainee is provided a written copy of the training program.	5	4	3	2	1
9. The trainer is provided a written copy of the training program.	5	4	3	2	1
10. Each customer-service skill to be learned is outlined in how-to steps.	5	4	3	2	1

ASSESSMENT SCALE (continued)

	Yes	Fairly Well	Some-what	Barely	No
11. A caring atmosphere of support is established with the trainee.	5	4	3	2	1
12. The standard of what constitutes an excellent job is spelled out for each customer-service task or skill to be learned.	5	4	3	2	1
13. Trainees are tested on required job knowledge.	5	4	3	2	1
14. Trainees are tested on required job behavior skills	5	4	3	2	1
15. The trainee is provided a continuous flow of feedback on progress.	5	4	3	2	1
16. The accomplishments of the trainee are recognized at the completion of critical learning steps.	5	4	3	2	1
17. A system of recording and tracking trainee progress is used.	5	4	3	2	1
18. Managers and supervisors are involved in the customer-service training process.	5	4	3	2	1
19. Customer-service trainers are trained in how to train.	5	4	3	2	1
20. Special customer-service training aids and/or manuals are available for the trainer.	5	4	3	2	1

SCORING INSTRUCTIONS:
Total the numbers circled. Your total score reflects your customer-service training program grade.

A = 100,   B = 80-89,   C = 70-79,   D = 60-69,   F = 59 and below

STEP 5

BUILD A WINNING TEAM WITH QUALITY CUSTOMER-SERVICE LEADERSHIP

"There must be a customer-oriented culture in the organization, and it is the leader of the enterprise who must build and maintain this culture."

Karl Albrecht/Ron Zemke
Service America

BUILDING A WINNING TEAM WITH QUALITY LEADERSHIP

THE WAY CUSTOMER-SERVICE EMPLOYEES ARE TREATED BY ORGANIZATIONAL LEADERS GREATLY IMPACTS HOW CUSTOMERS ARE TREATED BY THE ENTIRE ORGANIZATION.

The bottom line is...
> *YOUR SKILL AS A LEADER HAS A GREAT IMPACT ON HOW YOUR CUSTOMER SERVICE-TEAM TREATS YOUR CUSTOMERS!*

A FORMULA FOR QUALITY CUSTOMER-SERVICE LEADERSHIP

The leadership formula presented on the following two pages consists of five foundations. Each foundation builds on the other, creating a conceptual pyramid. Beginning at the bottom of the pyramid with the first foundation and moving to the one at the top, a leadership snowball effect is produced. Although each of the five foundations is considered separate and distinct from management skills, the leadership formula builds sound management principles along side of each ascending leadership foundation. *LEADERSHIP IS DEPENDENT ON A SOLID MANAGEMENT BASE.* You may be able to excel as a manager without becoming a quality leader, but cannot become a quality leader without also being an effective manager.

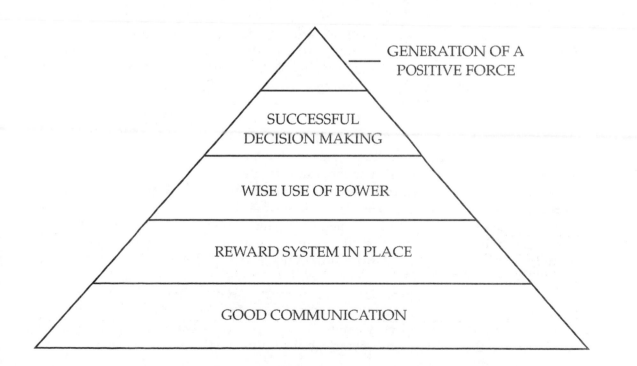

GENERATION OF A POSITIVE FORCE

SUCCESSFUL DECISION MAKING

WISE USE OF POWER

REWARD SYSTEM IN PLACE

GOOD COMMUNICATION

FIVE FOUNDATIONS TO CUSTOMER-SERVICE LEADERSHIP

FIRST FOUNDATION: QUALITY CUSTOMER-SERVICE LEADERS ARE EXTRAORDINARILY GOOD COMMUNICATORS

Managers must communicate to be effective in their jobs, but it's HOW they communicate that ultimately moves managers into the realm of leadership. Quality leaders not only seem to have the ability to express thought well—to speak and write clearly—they also have the ability to communicate forcefully in a "take-charge" manner, whether the group is large or small. They communicate with style and at the same time keep their followers well-informed. They also are superior listeners. This enables them to really understand what their followers want and need.

SECOND FOUNDATION: QUALITY CUSTOMER-SERVICE LEADERS PROVIDE THE RIGHT REWARDS TO THEIR CUSTOMER-SERVICE TEAM MEMBERS

There has to be something for the followers in the leader-follower dynamic. If not, followers will simply give their support to someone else. Quality customer-service leaders know what their team members want, and provide it. Because of their solid communication and listening skills, they are sensitive to and understand what it is that their followers really want. The right rewards include the right kind of reward, as well as the right amount at the right time.

Successful leaders of customer-service know that rewards flow in both directions. Service team members, in turn, provide rewards to leaders through their support, loyalty and performance. Quality leaders understand that they cannot expect to get and get and get without giving something back.

THIRD FOUNDATION: QUALITY CUSTOMER-SERVICE LEADERS USE POWER EFFECTIVELY

Power goes with leadership. Regardless of the base of a leader's power, quality leaders use that power with sensitivity and thoughtfulness. Power is never flaunted for its own sake, but used as a tool to maintain standards, establish structure, and accomplish goals. This allows quality leaders to win–but never at the expense of their service team members. This requires getting tough when getting tough is necessary. It requires setting an authority line that is clear, consistent and appropriate for the situation.

When power is used appropriately it is respected and welcomed by followers. This accepting attitude toward the use of power does not just happen. The groundwork must be laid very carefully through strong communication skills and provide the right mix of rewards to the entire customer-service team.

FIVE FOUNDATIONS (Continued)

FOURTH FOUNDATION:	**QUALITY CUSTOMER-SERVICE LEADERS ARE SUCCESSFUL DECISION MAKERS**

Outstanding quality leaders do not shy away from making decisions. In fact, the strongest leaders tend to measure their strength by the extent of their successful decision making track record. Quality leaders are made by their ability to make the right decision at the right time. Making right decisions, in turn, increases the service team's support for their leader.

Quality leaders tend to avoid off-the-cuff or gut-level decisions. They know when to involve others in the decision-making process, but tend not to allow getting bogged down in participatory decision making for its own sake. Interestingly, quality leaders also understand the need to change course as soon as possible when a misjudgment has been made. They are able to admit mistakes and get on with the business at hand.

Leaders of customer-service enterprises are often subject to a great deal of pressure from all sides when making decisions. Their decision may not be liked by all. Consequently, effective decision making requires inner strength and courage.

FIFTH FOUNDATION:	**QUALITY CUSTOMER-SERVICE LEADERS CREATE AND MAINTAIN A POSITIVE FORCE**

Acting as a positive force represent the apex of the quality leadership formula. This is the most difficult foundation for a customer-service leader to accomplish on a sustaining basis. This foundation is much more elusive, more abstract than the other foundations. Yet, quality leaders are able to generate a contagious positive force. Leaders of quality set an active tempo that others try to emulate. They are able to send positive rays of energy in all directions. Quality leaders transmit vigor, vitality as well as a sense of accomplishment and purpose—through good times and bad—for they realize that others are looking to them for guidance and direction.

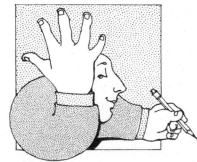

FIVE FOUNDATIONS FOR SUCCESS

HOW DO YOU RATE YOUR LEADERSHIP ABILITY

RESPOND TO THE CUSTOMER-SERVICE LEADERSHIP EFFECTIVENESS SCALE AND FIND OUT!

> *Recommended procedure:* Rate yourself as a leader first. Then invite other people who know you well in your customer-service work environment to respond to the "Customer-Service Leadership Effectiveness Scale" with you in mind. From your own input and theirs, you should be able to arrive at a fairly accurate profile of your leadership strengths and weaknesses. From there, formulate an action plan for improvement.

---

*For a complete discussion of the leadership formula see, Elwood N. Chapman, *Put More Leadership into Your Style*. Chicago, Ill: Science Research Associates, 1984.

CUSTOMER-SERVICE LEADERSHIP EFFECTIVENESS SCALE

INSTRUCTIONS

This instrument describes thirty (30) practices that are commonly demonstrated by acknowledged leaders. Please read each statement carefully. Then decide the extent to which you demonstrate that practice. Indicate your decision by circling the appropriate code to the right of each practice.

The person being rated:	Usually if not Always	Fairly Often	Occa-sionally	Rarely if Ever
1. Keeps group members informed.	U/A	FO	OC	R/E
2. Expresses thoughts clearly and forcefully.	U/A	FO	OC	R/E
3. Speaks well from a platform.	U/A	FO	OC	R/E
4. Is a poor listener.	U/A	FO	OC	R/E
5. Attracts others to want to hear what he or she has to say.	U/A	FO	OC	R/E
6. Communicates a sense of "being in charge."	U/A	FO	OC	R/E
7. Encourages upward communication from followers.	U/A	FO	OC	R/E
8. Demonstrates little compassion for others.	U/A	FO	OC	R/E
9. Provides rewards that are important to followers.	U/A	FO	OC	R/E
10. Is insensitive to the needs of others.	U/A	FO	OC	R/E
11. Attracts others to want to join his or her group.	U/A	FO	OC	R/E
12. Has the full backing of all those who work under him or her.	U/A	FO	OC	R/E
13. Provides enough structure to create a cohesive feeling among his or her subordinates.	U/A	FO	OC	R/E
14. Establishes an authority line that is clear, consistent, and appropriate for the situation.	U/A	FO	OC	R/E

(Continued on next page)

LEADERSHIP EFFECTIVENESS SCALE (CONTINUED)

The person being rated:

	Usually if not Always	Fairly Often	Occa-sionally	Rarely if Ever
15. Strives to win at the expense of subordinates.	U/A	FO	OC	R/E
16. Gets tough when necessary.	U/A	FO	OC	R/E
17. Loses respect from subordinates when authority is used.	U/A	FO	OC	R/E
18. Uses the power that he or she has with firmness but also with sensitivity.	U/A	FO	OC	R/E
19. Consults with others before making important decisions.	U/A	FO	OC	R/E
20. Has a strong track record for making solid decisions.	U/A	FO	OC	R/E
21. Follows no logical pattern in making decisions.	U/A	FO	OC	R/E
22. Communicates decisions with pride and decisiveness.	U/A	FO	OC	R/E
23. Finds it difficult to admit mistakes when he or she makes them.	U/A	FO	OC	R/E
24. Faces up to and makes hard decisions.	U/A	FO	OC	R/E
25. Gets others caught up in his or her positive force.	U/A	FO	OC	R/E
26. Creates an active tempo that others emulate.	U/A	FO	OC	R/E
27. Communicates a negative attitude through difficult or tough times.	U/A	FO	OC	R/E
28. Always puts his or her best foot forward.	U/A	FO	OC	R/E
29. Articulates an inspiring mission for the group.	U/A	FO	OC	R/E
30. Generates a feeling of pride and accomplishment in his or her followers.	U/A	FO	OC	R/E

LEADERSHIP EFFECTIVENESS SCALE (CONTINUED)

Scoring Instructions: Determine the point value for your response to each item and enter it in the score column. Total the scores for all six items in each category to obtain the CATEGORY SCORE. Then, enter the scores for each category in the SCORE column of the summary section. Total the category scores to obtain your CUSTOMER-SERVICE LEADERSHIP EFFECTIVENESS SCORE.

1. Leader as COMMUNICATOR:

Item:	U/A	FO	OC	R/E	Score
1.	4	3	2	1	____
2.	4	3	2	1	____
3.	4	3	2	1	____
4.	1	2	3	4	____
5.	4	3	2	1	____
6.	4	3	2	1	____
Category Score =					_____

2. Leader as MUTUAL REWARDER:

Item:	U/A	FO	OC	R/E	Score
7.	4	3	2	1	____
8.	1	2	3	4	____
9.	4	3	2	1	____
10.	1	2	3	4	____
11.	4	3	2	1	____
12.	4	3	2	1	____
Category Score =					_____

3. Leader as POWER FIGURE:

Item:	U/A	FO	OC	R/E	Score
13.	4	3	2	1	____
14.	4	3	2	1	____
15.	1	2	3	4	____
16.	4	3	2	1	____
17.	1	2	3	4	____
18.	4	3	2	1	____
Category Score =					_____

4. Leader as DECISION MAKER:

Item:	U/A	FO	OC	R/E	Score
19.	4	3	2	1	____
20.	4	3	2	1	____
21.	1	2	3	4	____
22.	4	3	2	1	____
23.	1	2	3	4	____
24.	4	3	2	1	____
Category Score =					_____

5. Leader as POSITIVE FORCE:

Item:	U/A	FO	OC	R/E	Score
25.	4	3	2	1	____
26.	4	3	2	1	____
27.	1	2	3	4	____
28.	4	3	2	1	____
29.	4	3	2	1	____
30.	4	3	2	1	____
Category Score =					_____

TOTALS	SCORE
1. COMMUNICATOR	____
2. MUTUAL REWARDER	____
3. POWER FIGURE	____
4.DECISION MAKER	____
5. POSITIVE FORCE	____
TOTAL: CUSTOMER-SERVICE LEADERSHIP EFFECTIVENESS SCORE	____

Score Interpretation
120-105 = quality leader,   104-90 = good leader,   89-75 = fair leader

STEP 6

BUILD A WINNING TEAM WITH A SUPPORTIVE ORGANIZATIONAL CLIMATE

The atmosphere within a work environment can be described in similar ways to the earth's atmosphere. A particular region of the globe may have good weather or bad weather from day-to-day just as an organization may have some good days and some bad days. Yet most regions of the globe have fairly predictable climates, from season to season. Organizations are no different.

One organizational climate may be described as strife ridden and stormy while another may be peaceful and calm. Some organizational climates are static while others are dynamic. Organizational climates can also be *SUPPORTIVE* or *NONSUPPORTIVE* of quality customer service.

Unlike the weather, organizational climate can be controlled. It can be made better, or worse, by the actions of leaders as well as employees.

Every organization has its own unique traditions, culture, and ways of getting things done. This includes how customers are treated. Climates may vary from organization to organization; however, there are some common identifiable features of organizational climate that serve to support quality customer service.

QUALITY CUSTOMER SERVICE TENDS TO THRIVE IN SOME CLIMATES AND WITHER IN OTHERS.

HOW SUPPORTIVE IS YOUR ORGANIZATIONAL CLIMATE?

DOES IT PROVIDE A FERTILE ENVIRONMENT FOR QUALITY CUSTOMER SERVICE?

"As a manager, the important thing is not what happens when you are there but what happens when you are not there."

Kenneth Blanchard/Robert Lorber
Putting the One-Minute Manager to Work

CUSTOMER SERVICE CLIMATE ASSESSMENT SCALE

Rate the organizational climate in which you work on how supportive it is of efforts to provide quality customer service. Circle your response to each question.

		LO				HI
1.	What is the level of employee commitment to organizational goals?	1	2	3	4	5
2.	How much group cohesion and interaction exists within work groups?	1	2	3	4	5
3.	To what extent do employees help and support each other voluntarily?	1	2	3	4	5
4.	How much opportunity is available for employees to develop new skills and knowledge?	1	2	3	4	5
5.	How much involvement and influence do employees have in decisions that affect their jobs?	1	2	3	4	5
6.	To what extent are employees rewarded and advanced on the basis of ability, performance, and experience?	1	2	3	4	5
7.	To what extent can employees make progress toward career goals?	1	2	3	4	5
8.	What is the level of positive employee-supervisor relations as reflected in fairness, honesty, and mutual respect?	1	2	3	4	5
9.	To what extent does the organization treat individuals as adults, with respect and dignity?	1	2	3	4	5
10.	How much confidence do the employees have in management?	1	2	3	4	5
11.	To what extent do the physical working conditions provide a supportive work environment?	1	2	3	4	5
12.	What is the level of economic well-being among employees?	1	2	3	4	5
13.	How positive are employee attitudes toward their jobs?	1	2	3	4	5
14.	To what extent do positive working conditions reduce job stress in your work environment?	1	2	3	4	5
15.	To what extent does management and union recognize mutual goals and work well together?	1	2	3	4	5

SCORING THE CUSTOMER-SERVICE CLIMATE ASSESSMENT SCALE
Total all the numbers circled. **TOTAL SCORE** _____

SCORE INTERPRETATION:
75-71 VERY SUPPORTIVE
70-55 SUPPORTIVE
54-40 LITTLE SUPPORT
39-25 NONSUPPORTIVE
24-15 YOU'LL SOON BE OUT OF BUSINESS

REVIEW OF STAGE III

SIX STEPS ARE REQUIRED TO BUILD A WINNING CUSTOMER-SERVICE TEAM.

I. Design QUALITY into each customer JOB.

II. Write JOB SPECIFICATIONS using established quality customer-service STANDARDS.

III. Screen job APPLICANTS carefully for quality customer-service strengths and abilities.

IV. Use effective TRAINING to maximize the development of quality customer-service expectations and skills.

V. Practice the principles of LEADERSHIP that promote winning teams.

VI. Nurture an ORGANIZATIONAL CLIMATE that supports quality customer-service.

YOUR ACTION PLAN FOR STAGE III

After reviewing the six steps for building a winning customer-service team, what are YOU going to do NOW to implement these proven principles into your customer-service operation? Write a brief Action Plan in the space below.

_____

_____

_____

_____

_____

_____

_____

_____

_____

_____

_____

"YOU CAN DO IT!"

ACTION PLAN
1.
2.
3.

STAGE IV

CHECK UP REGULARLY

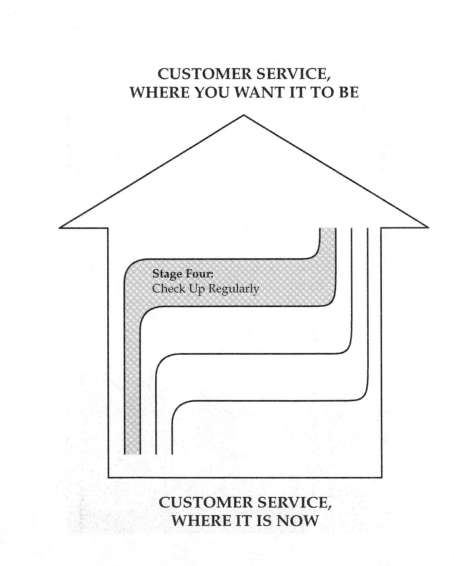

**CUSTOMER SERVICE,
WHERE YOU WANT IT TO BE**

Stage Four:
Check Up Regularly

**CUSTOMER SERVICE,
WHERE IT IS NOW**

CHECK REGULARLY ON HOW YOU ARE DOING

Up to this point in the book, we hope you have become more aware of what you can do as a manager of customer-service to clarify and improve your service image. Two powerful ways to do that include *SETTING SERVICE STANDARDS* and *BUILDING A WINNING CUSTOMER-SERVICE TEAM*.

ONCE YOU HAVE DEVELOPED A SHARP QUALITY CUSTOMER-SERVICE IMAGE, YOU MUST WORK TO MAINTAIN IT.

AN EFFECTIVE WAY TO MAINTAIN THE SERVICE IMAGE YOU HAVE WORKED TO CREATE IS TO DEVELOP A SYSTEM TO MONITOR THE PERFORMANCE OF YOUR CUSTOMER-SERVICE TEAM.

YOUR MEASUREMENT SYSTEM

CHECKING UP ON YOUR SERVICE DELIVERY PERFORMANCE REQUIRES AN ON-GOING SYSTEM OF—

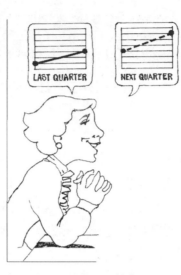

MEASUREMENT

This stage reviews three measurement systems you can use to check up on the quality of the service you and your service team render.

(1) A SERVICE AUDIT SYSTEM

Which allows you to focus on the key indicators of quality service

(2) A CUSTOMER FEEDBACK SYSTEM

Which enhances customer accessibility on an on-going basis

(3) AN EMPLOYEE FEEDBACK SYSTEM

Which keeps the entire team on track and headed in the right direction

CHECK ON HOW YOU'RE DOING WITH A SERVICE AUDIT

> "...The service audit, and a process for measuring quality service and feeding back this information to the frontline people are crucial ingredients in moving an organization to a high level of service orientation."
>
> Karl Albrecht/Ron Zemke
> *Service America*

CREATING A SERVICE AUDIT

What Is A Service Audit?
A service audit is a structured format for determining on a regular basis how your service delivery system is functioning. It establishes a way of measuring the success of your service delivery system.

How Does A Service Audit Work?
A service audit identifies the important OBSERVABLE KEY INDICATORS of quality customer service.

The service audit is facilitated by a check sheet or rating form that outlines the targeted key indicators of quality service. This form identifies the areas most critical to successful delivery.

A manager, or service auditor, uses the rating form when reviewing the service operation on a regular periodic basis.

How Is A Service Audit Form Created?
If you have developed a listing of measurable indicators of your quality service standards as outlined in Stage Two of this book, you are well on your way to creating a workable service audit system.

You should use your measurable/observable indicators of quality service standards as a point of reference.

The next step is for you to get together with a task force of talented and experienced service managers to generate a single page list of KEY INDICATORS of quality service delivery.

After that, develop (1) a RATING SCALE which facilitates the recording of the *frequency of occurrence* of each indicator and (2) make a place on the form to record the frequency of observed behavior.

CREATING A SERVICE AUDIT
(Continued)

Advantages of a Service Audit

A service audit requires MBWA, "Management By Walking Around." It demands that managers be out where the action is. Auditing requires careful observation, examination, and scrutiny of each service step and function. It provides a focus for the managers who are walking around. It helps management look at the actions most critical to service success, focus discussion of these things, and reinforce and reward these same behaviors that generate quality customer service.

WARNING

Dangers of A Service Audit System
A dangerous misuse of a service audit is using it as a vehicle to criticize and cast blame instead of using it to identify and reinforce *desirable* behavior.

THE SERVICE AUDIT FORM IS DESIGNED TO MEASURE HOW WELL YOU ARE DOING...NOT HOW POORLY.

A service audit system is intended to highlight and reinforce desired behavior. Therefore,

THE BEST USE OF A SERVICE AUDIT SYSTEM IS TO IDENTIFY, RECOGNIZE, AND REWARD QUALITY SERVICE BEHAVIOR. ITS PURPOSE IS TO HELP CATCH PEOPLE DOING SOMETHING RIGHT. IT SHOULD BE USED TO GIVE A PAT ON THE BACK.

Once the service audit process takes on a "policing" function it generates distrust and defensiveness. This, in turn, destroys the open and trusting climate necessary for the health and survival of quality customer service.

THE EXAMPLE OF THE FACING PAGE OF A SERVICE AUDIT FORM IS FOR AN AIRLINE FLIGHT ATTENDANT CREW. SEVERAL EXAMPLES OF KEY INDICATORS OF QUALITY SERVICE ARE SHOWN FOR SELECTED QUALITY SERVICE STANDARDS.

EXAMPLE SERVICE AUDIT FORM

> Targeted Customer-Service Team: Flight Attendant Crew
>
> Measurement Scale: 2 = Above Standard
>   1 = At Standard
>   0 = Below Standard
>   N/O = Not Observed

Timeliness

____ Beverage service is completed 40 minutes after take off.

____ Complete meal service is completed in $1\frac{1}{2}$ to $1\frac{3}{4}$ hours.

Organized Flow

____ Passengers are assisted with stowage of baggage when they are having difficulty.

____ The crew members overlap duties when problems arise in the cabin and galleys.

Accommodation

____ Passengers who wish to disembark first due to urgent reasons are seated next to the exit of disembarkation before landing whenever possible.

____ Requests to change seats, within the ticketed travel class are accommodated whenever possible.

Anticipation

____ Parents with infants are informed of changing tables in the toilets.

____ Passengers are offered beverage refills without having to ask for them.

Communication

____ Pre-flight instructions are heard clearly throughout the cabin.

____ Passengers are informed of relevant details regarding flight departure and arrival.

SAMPLE SERVICE AUDIT FORM
(Continued)

Tone of Voice

_____ Flight attendants indicate interest in conversation with passengers by varying their tone of voice.

_____ Flight attendants exhibit a friendly, relaxed tone of voice.

Body Language

_____ Flight attendants greet passengers with a friendly, welcoming smile.

_____ Flight attendants talk with passengers eye to eye.

Attentiveness

_____ Unaccompanied minors are checked on regularly and helped with meals, as age requires.

_____ Flight attendants pull down window shades for passengers who have fallen asleep.

Tact

_____ Passengers are called by surname in first class seats.

_____ Child passengers are addressed by their first name.

Guidance

_____ The menu is explained to passengers.

_____ Menu alternatives are mentioned to passengers not eating the main meal.

Gracious Problem Solving

_____ Flight attendants listen patiently and express empathy to all complaints and problems expressed by passengers and attempt, when possible, to personally see to the passengers' satisfaction.

_____ The lead flight attendant personally talks with every complaining passenger during the flight.

CHECK ON HOW YOU ARE DOING WITH A CUSTOMER FEEDBACK SYSTEM

*HELLO, I'M CONDUCTING A FOLLOW-UP
TO THE SERVICE YOU RECEIVED FROM OUR COMPANY."*

CREATING A CUSTOMER FEEDBACK SYSTEM

What Is A Customer Feedback System?
A customer feedback system is an *organized and deliberate* way of finding out what your customers think about the job you are doing. This requires that customer feedback is not left to chance or fate. It is not collected haphazardly, and it is proactive, not reactive. It is planned and organized, with the intention of optimizing customer information flow into the organization.

What Does A Customer Feedback System Tell You?
Customer feedback systems can provide answers to the following questions:

To what extent are your customers satisfied?

What do they REALLY think?

What do they like about your service?

What do they dislike?

What are their most common complaints?

What suggestions do they have for improving your service?

FINDING ANSWERS TO THESE QUESTIONS CAN BE QUITE DIFFICULT BECAUSE:

> –MOST CUSTOMERS DO NOT LIKE TO COMPLAIN, and if they do have a complaint,
>
> –TOO MANY CUSTOMERS CHOOSE NOT TO TAKE THE TIME AND ENERGY TO PROVIDE POSITIVE FEEDBACK.

FEEDBACK ROADBLOCKS

ROADBLOCKS TO CUSTOMER FEEDBACK

MANY CUSTOMERS DO NOT COMPLAIN BECAUSE OF TWO ROAD-BLOCKS:

1) They don't believe it will make a difference, AND

2) They don't have easy access to you.

IN ADDITION, TOO MANY CUSTOMERS FAIL TO SHARE POSITIVE EXPE-RIENCES WITH YOU BECAUSE OF THE SAME TWO ROADBLOCKS:

1) They don't believe it will make a difference, AND

2) They don't have easy access to you.

ROADBLOCK I. *Customers don't believe feedback makes a difference.*
Many have been burned in the past. Too often in response to a complaint, they are confronted with apathy, out-and-out hostility, no response, a slow response or "the polite form letter." And at other times when organizations respond with receptivity and politeness to a customer's remarks, nothing seems to change on the frontlines. Consequently, it is not surprising to see so many people refusing to invest time and energy in an endeavor that yields so little payback.

ROADBLOCK II. *Customers don't have access to the people who can make a difference.*
All too often, customer-service organizations make it extremely difficult for their customers to access the people who can make a difference. Too many times they are forced to interact with a low-level employee who has little or no influence or authority within the organization. At other times, they may be faced with a web of screening secretaries with the results that the person to whom they need to talk to is "unavailable."

WHAT CAN YOU DO TO ELIMINATE THESE ROADBLOCKS?

YOU LIFT THE ROADBLOCKS TO CUSTOMER FEEDBACK WHEN YOU–

I. DEMONSTRATE BY YOUR ACTIONS THAT YOU ARE REALLY LISTENING TO THEM.

II. MAKE IT EASY FOR CUSTOMERS TO SHARE INFORMATION WITH YOU, AND

INVITE FEEDBACK

SOME SUGGESTIONS ON HOW TO DO THIS CAN BE FOUND THE NEXT PAGE.

CUSTOMER FEEDBACK (Continued)

TEN WAYS TO OPEN UP CUSTOMER ACCESS TO YOUR ORGANIZATION

1. Get out and talk person-to-person with your customers. Spend some time with them. Get to know them. TALK WITH THEM.

2. Organize focus groups. Invite selected customers to come in and discuss what they like and dislike in a open forum.

3. Ask customers to respond to a customer survey, over the phone, through the mail, or in person.

4. Have suggestion boxes and feedback forms available in strategic places–where your customers are.

5. Find out where the problems lie and fix them. Tell your customers what you have done to fix them.

6. Initiate a customer newsletter or other communication device to broadcast how much you want their input and just how you are responding to it.

7. Move customer-service communication and complaint handling from a low position in the organization to one with clout.

8. Respond, respond, respond and RAPIDLY to all customer complaints and requests.

9. Provide customer help and encouragement in processing refunds, exchanges, and complaints (i.e., have a toll free phone number for customer assistance and information).

10. Measure and evaluate managers' performance on the ability to access customer feedback.

11. ADD YOUR OWN IDEAS: _____

    _____

    _____

CREATING AN EMPLOYEE FEEDBACK SYSTEM

WHAT IS AN EMPLOYEE FEEDBACK SYSTEM?

An employee feedback system is an organized way of noting employee job performance *behavior* and *sharing* that information with the employee. It is a system whereby you and your employees can *mutually* check on the quality level of customer service as performed by the employee.

An employee feedback system that supports quality customer service focuses on *(1) CUSTOMER-SERVICE BEHAVIOR, (2) SHARING OF INFORMATION* and *(3) A MUTUAL GIVE AND TAKE OF IDEAS.*

BEHAVIOR: A customer-service employee feedback system must focus on what the employees *DO*, how they *ACT*, and what they *SAY* that produces defined, observable and measurable results. It is NOT a time to dwell on intangible personality characteristics. The behavior that you are after must be *JOB RE-LATED* and *REFLECT YOUR QUALITY CUSTOMER-SERVICE STANDARDS* generated in Stage II.

SHARING: Employee feedback systems do nothing to reinforce desirable customer-service behaviors unless customer-service employees are fully aware, at all times, how they are doing in the eyes of management. This is the principle of *"NO SURPRISES."* When you follow this principle, you make sure that all information regarding employee productivity and performance is readily and openly shared with employees.

MUTUAL GIVE AND TAKE: An employee feedback system that works is NOT one where the boss does all the talking or whose perceptions are always right. An employee feedback system that supports quality customer service must allow and nurture a *TWO-WAY* exchange of ideas and perceptions between the manager and customer-service employee.

> "Feedback is the Breakfast of Champions."
> Kenneth Blanchard/Robert Lorber
> *Putting the One-Minute Manager to Work*

THREE WAYS YOU CAN PROVIDE FEEDBACK TO CUSTOMER-SERVICE EMPLOYEES:

I. PROVIDE DAILY VERBAL FEEDBACK REGARDING CUSTOMER-SERVICE SUCCESS ON AN INDIVIDUAL BASIS TO YOUR CUSTOMER-SERVICE EMPLOYEES,

II. POST MEASURES OF INDIVIDUAL AND GROUP CUSTOMER-SERVICE PRODUCTIVITY

and

III. CONDUCT PERIODIC PERFORMANCE AND APPRAISALS BASED ON MEASURABLE/OBSERVABLE QUALITY CUSTOMER-SERVICE STANDARDS

HOW NOT TO OBTAIN FEEDBACK

I. PROVIDE DAILY VERBAL EMPLOYEE FEEDBACK

"Feedback is an essential ingredient of coaching, counseling, performance appraisal, and all day-to-day conversations with an employee. It is an ongoing activity through which an employee is kept constantly aware of his performance and any changes needed or expected."

James F. Evered
Shirt-Sleeves Management

THE PRINCIPLE OF NO SURPRISES

The principle of "no surprises" is based on the simple fact that information is power and the most powerful information is positive information. When you share positive information with your employees, you are generating a powerful influence on their job behavior. Simply put, positive reinforcement increases the frequency of a desired response. When a behavior is followed by no information or negative information, that behavior tends to occur less and less frequently. However, when you focus on positive information you not only create a supportive work climate but also reinforce desired quality customer-service behaviors.

TALK TO YOUR EMPLOYEES AS MUCH AS POSSIBLE. LET THEM KNOW WHAT THEY ARE DOING RIGHT—EVERYDAY!

Nothing is more effective as a reinforcer of quality customer service as a genuine pat on the back and a congratulations of a "job well done." This should be done verbally and it should be done daily. The power is dramatic. It generates pride, self-esteem and a feeling that someone cares. It builds a strong, cohesive customer-service team. In short, it works.

AS A MANAGER OF CUSTOMER-SERVICE, VERBALLY RECOGNIZING QUALITY CUSTOMER-SERVICE BEHAVIOR ON A DAILY BASIS IS BY FAR THE SINGLE MOST IMPORTANT THING YOU CAN DO TO REINFORCE AND SUPPORT QUALITY CUSTOMER-SERVICE BEHAVIORS IN YOUR EMPLOYEES.

II. POST MEASURES OF INDIVIDUAL AND GROUP CUSTOMER-SERVICE PRODUCTIVITY

Performance feedback must be provided to all customer-service employees on a *continuous basis*. Lack of feedback eventually leads to the extinction of the customer-service behaviors you desire. Your customer-service employees need information fed back to them on their level of performance.

This book has emphasized the power of positive feedback to reinforce the behavior you want.

ONE WAY TO DO THIS IS TO POST CHARTS AND GRAPHS OF CUSTOMER-SERVICE PERFORMANCE.

ADVANTAGES of posting customer-service productivity.

GRAPHS AND CHARTS PROVIDE–

- A visual "score" of how well you are doing.
- A record of progress over time.
- An easy means of establishing targets or goals.
- A comparison with other individuals or groups.
- An opportunity to recognize excellence.

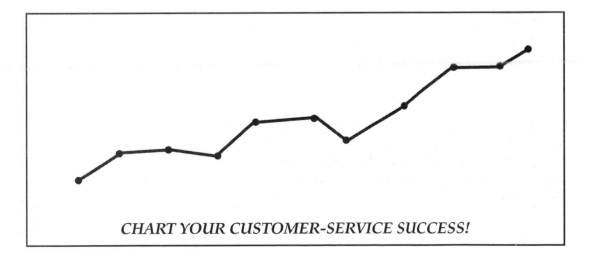

CHART YOUR CUSTOMER-SERVICE SUCCESS!

GRAPHIC FACTS

- A VISUAL PRESENTATION OF SUCCESS IS WORTH MORE THAN A THOUSAND WORDS.

- THE RESULTS ON A CHART SPEAK FOR THEMSELVES.

- CHARTS HELP YOU MAKE A DRAMATIC STATEMENT ABOUT YOUR PROGRESS IN CUSTOMER SERVICE.

- A CHART MAKES IT CLEAR TO ALL WHAT YOUR GOALS ARE.

- A CHART HELPS SET A COMMON DIRECTION FOR ALL TO WORK TOWARD.

WHAT CAN YOU CHART?

HERE ARE A FEW EXAMPLES:

1. Individual or group sales efforts for a selected period of time (average sales, total sales, etc.)

2. Number of new customers served

3. Number of total customers served

4. Number of letters of commendation

5. Number of customer complaints

6. Customer surveys scores

7. Shopper report results

8. Service audit scores

9. Measures of speed and efficiency of service

10. ADD YOUR OWN: _____

III. CONDUCT PERIODIC PERFORMANCE APPRAISALS USING QUALITY CUSTOMER-SERVICE STANDARDS

As we have tried to make poignantly clear in this section of the book, commendable job performance should be verbally recognized on a daily basis. Beyond this, however, you should conduct sit-down performance appraisals on a regular three-to-six month basis with all customer-service employees.

These sessions should be conducted in a non-threatening environment with an EMPHASIS ON SPECIFIC, QUALITY CUSTOMER-SERVICE BEHAVIORS relative to SPECIFIC QUALITY CUSTOMER-SERVICE STANDARDS.

HERE IS A CHECK LIST YOU CAN USE FOR CONDUCTING YOUR CUSTOMER-SERVICE PERFORMANCE APPRAISALS.

The check list on the following pages is designed to guide you in

(1) PREPARING,

(2) CONDUCTING, and

(3) FOLLOWING THROUGH

WITH CUSTOMER-SERVICE EMPLOYEE PERFORMANCE APPRAISAL DISCUSSIONS.*

---

* This material has been adapted from *Effective Performance Appraisals*, a Crisp Publication written by Robert B. Maddux.

PERFORMANCE APPRAISAL CHECKLIST

I. PERSONAL PREPARATION

❏ I have reviewed mutually understood customer-service job duties, goals, and quality performance standards for the person under review.

❏ I have observed the job performance of this person measures against mutually understood customer-service expectations. In so doing, I have done my best to avoid such pitfalls as:

❏ Bias/prejudice.
❏ The vagaries of memory.
❏ Over attention to some aspects of the job at the expense of others.
❏ Being overly influenced by my own experience.
❏ Trait evaluation rather than performance measurement.

❏ I have reviewed the employee's background including:

❏ Skills.
❏ Work experience.
❏ Training.

❏ I have determined the employee's performance strengths and areas in need of improvement and in so doing have:

❏ Accumulated specific, unbiased documentation that can be used to help communicate my position.
❏ Limited myself to those critical points that are the most important.
❏ Prepared a possible development plan in case the employee needs assistance in coming up with a suitable plan.

❏ I have identified areas for concentration in setting goals and standards for the next appraisal period.

❏ I have given the employee advance notice when the discussion will be held so that he or she can prepare.

❏ I have set aside an adequate block of uninterrupted time to permit a full and complete discussion.

PERFORMANCE APPRAISAL CHECKLIST (Continued)

II. CONDUCTING THE APPRAISAL DISCUSSION

❑ I plan to begin the discussion by creating a sincere, open and friendly atmosphere. This includes:

  ❑ Reviewing the purpose of the discussion.
  ❑ Making it clear that it is a joint discussion for the purpose of mutual problem solving and goal setting.
  ❑ Striving to put the employee at ease.

❑ In the body of the discussion I intend to keep the focus on job performance and related factors. This includes:

  ❑ Discussing job requirements—employee strengths, accomplishments, improvement needs—evaluating results of performance against objectives set during previous reviews and discussions.
  ❑ Being prepared to cite observations for each point I want to discuss.
  ❑ Encouraging the employee to appraise his or her own customer-service performance.
  ❑ Using open, reflective and directive questions to promote thought, understanding and problem solving.

❑ I will encourage the employee to outline his or her personal plans for self-development before suggesting ideas of my own. In the process, I will:

  ❑ Try to get the employee to set personal growth and improvement targets.
  ❑ Strive to reach agreement on appropriate development plans that detail what the employee intends to do, a time table and support I am prepared to give.

❑ I am prepared to discuss work assignments, projects and goals for the next appraisal period and will ask the employee to come prepared with suggestions.

❑ I will be prepared to make notes during the discussion for the purpose of summarizing agreements and follow up. In closing, I will:

  ❑ Summarize what has been discussed.
  ❑ Show enthusiasm for plans that have been made.
  ❑ Give the employee an opportunity to make additional suggestions.
  ❑ End on a positive, friendly, harmonious note.

APPRAISAL FOLLOW-UP

III. FOLLOW THROUGH AFTER THE APPRAISAL

❑ As soon as the discussion is over, I will record the plans made, points requiring follow up, the commitments I made, and provide a copy for the employee.

❑ I will also evaluate how I handled the discussion.

❑ What I did well.
❑ What I could have done better.
❑ What I learned about the employee and his or her job.
❑ What I learned about myself and my job.

REVIEW OF STAGE IV

To succeed at this stage, you must have an on-going system of measuring customer-service progress. Here are three measurement systems you can put to use in your operation.

A. A SERVICE AUDIT SYSTEM

A service audit system involves using a structured check sheet or rating form consisting of selected observable/measurable key indicators of quality customer service. This form is to be used on a regular basis by a "service auditor" to measure the frequency of desired customer-service processes and outcomes.

B. A CUSTOMER FEEDBACK SYSTEM

A customer feedback system consists of an organized and systematic way of making it easy for customers to share information with you. Such a system should work to eliminate the common roadblocks to customer feedback. The actions you take in response to customer comments are critical to promoting more and better feedback from your customers.

C. AN EMPLOYEE FEEDBACK SYSTEM

An employee feedback system that works to encourage and reinforce quality customer service is (1) based on behavior, (2) utilizes the principles of "no surprises," and (3) requires a give and take between supervisors and employees. This kind of system makes use of daily, positive, verbal feedback, the posting of individual productivity scores, and conducting periodic performance appraisals based on customer-service standards.

YOUR ACTION PLAN FOR STAGE IV

After reviewing three effective measuring tools for checking on customer-service progress, what are YOU going to do *NOW* to put their power to work for you in your customer-service operation? Write a brief Action Plan in the space below.

_____

_____

_____

_____

_____

_____

_____

_____

_____

STAGE V

PROVIDE PROACTIVE PROBLEM SOLVING

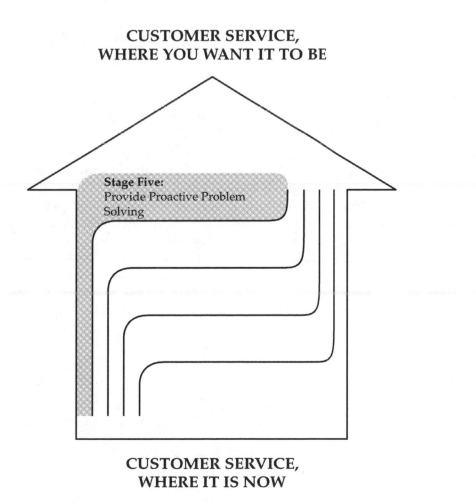

CUSTOMER SERVICE,
WHERE YOU WANT IT TO BE

Stage Five:
Provide Proactive Problem
Solving

CUSTOMER SERVICE,
WHERE IT IS NOW

PROVIDING PROACTIVE CUSTOMER-SERVICE PROBLEM SOLVING

The fifth stage in the customer-service management cycle focuses on four *ACTION PLANS* you can use to create a proactive approach to customer-service problem solving.

ACTION PLAN 1.   *CREATE A SUPPORTIVE CLIMATE FOR SOLVING CUSTOMER-SERVICE PROBLEMS.*

ACTION PLAN 2.   *USE YOUR CUSTOMER-SERVICE TEAMS TO IDENTIFY CUSTOMER-SERVICE PROBLEM AREAS.*

ACTION PLAN 3.   *MAKE YOUR CUSTOMER-SERVICE TEAM A RESOURCE FOR IMPROVING SERVICE.*

ACTION PLAN 4.   *TURN CUSTOMER PROBLEMS AND COMPLAINTS INTO OPPORTUNITIES FOR STRENGTHENING TIES WITH YOUR CUSTOMERS.*

The underlying premise of this stage is the customer-service management process **goes beyond just reacting** effectively to customer complaints. **A proactive strategy of building an on-going viable relationship with customers is advocated here. This means involving your entire service team in identifying and solving customer-service related problems. This approach will fundamentally affect how your customers are treated not just when problems arise, but on a day-to-day basis.**

<table>
<tr><td>

**ACTION
PLAN
1**

</td><td>

CREATE A SUPPORTIVE CLIMATE FOR SOLVING CUSTOMER-SERVICE PROBLEMS

</td></tr>
</table>

It is not unusual for well-intentioned managers of customer service to know what needs to be done to improve the customer-service delivery system and to act on that knowledge. Unfortunately, this approach tends to overlook the fact that anytime a solution is introduced into the system, *RESISTANCE TO CHANGE WILL UNDOUBTEDLY OCCUR.*

Just because YOU see a need for change, doesn't necessarily mean YOUR TEAM sees the same need. They may resist attempted solutions or changes to improve customer-service for the following reasons.

—DIFFERING PERCEPTIONS. Your individual service team members may differ in how they perceive the level of service currently being provided. They have a unique frame of reference through which they interpret what goes on around them. Simply put, they may see things differently than you.

—PREVIOUS BEHAVIOR EXPECTATIONS AND OLD HABITS. Your organizational behavior expectations—or norms—are the rules of behavior team members are expected to follow. Your team has worked together to reinforce and perpetuate these rules. Many have become habits of behavior. These behaviors often take on an importance of their own. Pre-existing norms, like old habits, can be hard to break.

—INTERESTS UNDER ATTACK. The team member interests that are most often perceived as threatened by a proposed change usually involve money, power and/or status. When any one or a combination of these interests are perceived to be threatened by a proposed change, resistance to that idea will blossom. When this happens, the issue is often perceived as one of "them" against "us."

 EACH OF THESE CAUSES OF RESISTANCE IS POTENTIALLY DAMAGING TO THE HEALTH AND CARE OF A SUPPORTIVE TEAM ATMOSPHERE FOR CUSTOMER-SERVICE PROBLEM SOLVING.

WHAT CAN YOU DO TO MINIMIZE THIS RESISTANCE?

ACTION PLAN 1 (CONTINUED)

TEN SUGGESTIONS FOR CREATING A SUPPORTIVE CLIMATE FOR SOLVING CUSTOMER-SERVICE PROBLEMS

---

1. Allow your service team members to join in the diagnostic efforts leading to AGREEMENT OF WHAT THE BASIC SERVICE PROBLEMS ARE.

2. INVOLVE your service team in suggesting what changes need to be made to improve customer service.

3. SHARE as much customer-service feedback INFORMATION with your team as possible.

4. Whenever possible, work toward generating solutions that REDUCE PRESENT JOB BURDENS.

5. Support solutions that are consistent with organizational VALUES AND CULTURE when you can.

6. IMPLEMENT solutions GRADUALLY OR INCREMENTALLY when changes are major or all-encompassing.

7. Be willing to shift gears when necessary. REMAIN FLEXIBLE during the implementation process.

8. Recognize that valid objections may emerge from team members. BE RESPONSIVE TO OBJECTIONS.

9. Provide plenty of FEEDBACK AND INFORMATION as you implement service improvement strategies.

10. Promote a climate of acceptance, support, and trust between you and the members of your customer-service team.

<table>
<tr><td>

**ACTION
PLAN
2**

</td><td>

USE YOUR CUSTOMER-SERVICE TEAM TO IDENTIFY CUSTOMER-SERVICE PROBLEM AREAS

</td></tr>
</table>

When you bring your service team(s) together for the purpose of solving problems in customer-service delivery, the first step should be to **PIN-POINT SPECIFIC PROBLEM AREAS.** "The Customer-Service Assessment Scale" will help you do this.

THE CUSTOMER-SERVICE ASSESSMENT SCALE

The "CUSTOMER-SERVICE ASSESSMENT SCALE" (CSAS) was developed to help a *specific* service team identify certain strengths and weaknesses within its operation. It consists of twenty items that describe selected characteristics of customer-service delivery systems. Half of the items reflect the procedural dimension of service and the other half relate to the personal dimension.

THE CSAS WAS DESIGNED FOR GROUP USE. Its purpose is for a *specific* service delivery team to analyze its own customer-service performance. When individual members respond to the scale, they are to evaluate the **TEAM AS A WHOLE**. This requires the respondent to "average" the sum of individual service behaviors within the group or to conceptualize a "total team" impact on the customer.

ANALYSIS OF CSAS RESULTS

Group discussion. After everyone of the individual team members has had a chance to respond to the CSAS, they should be brought together to discuss their individual responses and to generate a group listing of perceived strengths and weaknesses. (Strengths are those 3-5 items that received, overall, the highest scores. The weaknesses are those 3-5 items that received the lowest overall scores.)

Suggested group size. This procedure works best in groups of five to seven. When teams are larger than this, they can be divided into sub-groups. This facilitates group discussion and individual involvement. Each sub-group should generate its own listing of strengths and weaknesses. When this is done, the entire team should agree on its overall strengths and weaknesses by analyzing and discussing the various lists from the sub-groups.

CUSTOMER-SERVICE ASSESSMENT SCALE (CSAS)

Name of Group _____

With this group in mind, answer the following questions according to how often the behavior ACTUALLY occurs.

DOES THIS GROUP:	Always	Usually	Fairly Often	Occasionally	Rarely	Never
1. Work in an organized, systematic way?	5	4	3	2	1	0
2. Use tactful words and comments with customers?	5	4	3	2	1	0
3. Exhibit flexibility when responding to varying customer requests?	5	4	3	2	1	0
4. Display a positive attitude on the job?	5	4	3	2	1	0
5. Follow procedures that make service as convenient as possible for customers?	5	4	3	2	1	0
6. Call customers by name?	5	4	3	2	1	0
7. Exhibit a thorough knowledge of all available products and services?	5	4	3	2	1	0
8. Allow smiles to surface while getting things done?	5	4	3	2	1	0
9. Generate a constructive working relationship with supervisors and/ or subordinates?	5	4	3	2	1	0
10. Provide helpful suggestions to customers?	5	4	3	2	1	0

CSAS (Continued)

DOES THIS GROUP:	Always	Usually	Fairly Often	Occa-sionally	Rarely	Never
11. Communicate well with fellow employees?	5	4	3	2	1	0
12. Excel in selling abilities?	5	4	3	2	1	0
13. Provide service in a timely manner consistent with customer needs?	5	4	3	2	1	0
14. Not allow customers to feel neglected in the rush of other activities?	5	4	3	2	1	0
15. Seek feedback from customers?	5	4	3	2	1	0
16. Provide service that is beyond what customers expect?	5	4	3	2	1	0
17. Communicate well with customers?	5	4	3	2	1	0
18. Refuse to deal with customers in an aloof or condescending way?	5	4	3	2	1	0
19. Accurately anticipate and plan for meeting customer needs?	5	4	3	2	1	0
20. Graciously handle complaining and/or difficult customers to their satisfaction?	5	4	3	2	1	0

DEVELOPING ONE LIST OF TEAM STRENGTHS AND WEAKNESSES

After the service team rates itself on the CSAS, the responses are tallied to generate a listing of service strengths and deficiencies for that specific service team.

This process works well because the people who performing customer-service are providing an opportunity to analyze their own service behaviors. This makes them active participants in the process of their own team improvement. It gives them a chance to take an objective view of the level of service they are providing and to see how the other team members view things.

This process acts to reduce defensiveness and resistance among team members. It also helps develop their commitment to doing something about improving the deficient areas.

Note: You should list service *STRENGTHS* as well as weaknesses. It is important to recognize what the team is doing well—to see what it is doing right. In this way the emphasis is not entirely on the negative. Take some time and congratulate strong performance in areas that are well deserved.

SAMPLE LISTING OF CUSTOMER-SERVICE STRENGTHS AND WEAKNESSES FOR A CUSTOMER-SERVICE TEAM	
Service Strengths	**Service Weaknesses**
1. We work in an organized and systematic way.	1. We do not call customers by name.
2. There is a constructive working relationship with our supervisors.	2. We are not completely knowledgeable on all the available products and services available to customers.
3. We provide timely service consistent with customer needs.	3. We need to seek more feedback from customers.
4. We communicate well with customers.	4. We need to communicate better with our fellow team members.

<table>
<tr><td>

ACTION
PLAN
3

</td><td>

USE YOUR CUSTOMER-SERVICE TEAM AS A RESOURCE FOR IMPROVING SERVICE

</td></tr>
</table>

ONCE YOU HAVE USED THE CUSTOMER-SERVICE ASSESSMENTS SCALE TO CONSTRUCT A LIST OF TEAM STRENGTHS AND WEAKNESSES, *INVOLVE THE TEAM IN DECIDING WHAT CAN BE DONE TO STRENGTHEN AREAS OF WEAKNESS.*

Here are two optional processes for doing this.

> *TEAM PROBLEM-SOLVING PROCESS OPTION #1:*
> **THE NOMINAL GROUP PROCESS**

1. PICK THE TARGET PROBLEM: Identify the ONE area from the list of weaknesses that the team agrees is currently the highest priority problem.

2. LIST POSSIBLE SOLUTIONS: Ask each member of the team, WORKING ALONE, to develop a list of possible solutions to the targeted problem.

3. RECORD SOLUTION IDEAS: One at a time, each team member offers ONE item from his or her list in a round-robin manner. A designated individual records each idea on a master list in full view of the entire team.

   This round-robin process continues until ALL ITEMS ON EACH PERSON'S LIST have been recorded.

4. VOTE: Ask each team member to rank on an individual ballot his or her preference with respect to the priority or importance of the items appearing on the master list.

   NOTE: NO VERBAL INTERACTION IS ALLOWED DURING STEPS TWO TO FOUR. THE RESULTS OF THE VOTING ARE TABULATED AND THE SCORES ARE POSTED ON THE MASTER LIST.

5. DISCUSS: The merits of each item are discussed fully for clarification as well as evaluation.

6. FINAL VOTE: Ask each team member to rank the remaining items a second time. Tally the results and agree upon the selected solution(s).

ACTION PLAN 3 (Continued)

1. PICK THE TARGET PROBLEM: Identify the *ONE* area from the list of weaknesses that the team agrees is currently the highest priority problem.

2. FORM SUB-GROUPS: Divide the team into groups of 5-7. This number facilitates the brainstorming process.

3. REVIEW THE RULES OF BRAINSTORMING:
   1) The group is to generate as many solution ideas as possible in the amount of time provided.
   2) All ideas from the group members must be recorded in full view of the group.
   3) There can be *NO DISCUSSION* of suggested items during the time of brainstorming.
   4) All items must be accepted and recorded.

4. COMMENCE BRAINSTORMING: Sometimes it is helpful to establish a goal, i.e., at least 10 ideas must be recorded. To keep energy levels active, it may also be useful to set a time period of 10-15 minutes to complete the brainstorming step.

5. DISCUSSION: Once a full list of possible solutions has been generated, each group must go through the various ideas and discuss the *QUALITATIVE MERITS* of each item suggested. Solution criteria such as commitment and resources needed for implementation need to be discussed.

6. CHOOSING A SOLUTION: Once the merits of each item have been discussed within all the groups, each group presents one or two of their best ideas to the entire group. A master list of "best ideas" is developed for the entire team to see. Each one of these ideas is discussed in turn, and a solution or set of solutions are agreed upon by the team.

ACTION PLAN 4

TURN CUSTOMER PROBLEMS INTO OPPORTUNITIES FOR BETTER CUSTOMER-SERVICE

> "...There are two kinds of companies. The first, the most typical, views the complaint as a disease to be got over, with memory of the pain rapidly suppressed. The second...views the complaint as a luscious *golden opportunity*."
>
> Tom Peters/Nancy Austin
> *A Passion for Excellence*

A KNEE-JERK RESPONSE TO CUSTOMER-SERVICE COMPLAINTS

This type of response to customer-service complaints is strictly reactive in nature. Organizations that respond in this way are passive in their approach to solving customer related problems. They wait for problems to emerge and then handle them by either ignoring, deflecting, or otherwise paying little attention to them. Also falling into this category are organizations that talk a lot about the importance of customers, give it a lot of lip service, but really fail to constructively organize and implement strong ties to the customer or work in a concerted way to improve the customer-service delivery system.

A PROACTIVE RESPONSE TO CUSTOMER-SERVICE COMPLAINTS

In contrast to the knee-jerk response, organizations that exhibit a proactive approach to customer-service problem solving actually encourage and welcome customer complaints. They continually work to increase customer access by viewing this process in the broader sense of building stronger ties to the customer. This approach involves a conscientious, planned strategy of strengthening customer ties in all ways possible. It views customer complaints as opportunities rather than problems. Roots to common complaints and problems are ferreted out and the system actually improves in the process. When it comes to customer service, complacency or satisfaction with the status quo are nowhere to be found in the organization's vocabulary.

ACTION PLAN 4 (Continued)

A PROACTIVE VIEW OF CUSTOMER COMPLAINTS

1. Complaints are welcome. Without them we can't improve.

2. We learn from complaints.

3. We must make it as easy as possible for customers to complain to us.

4. We take our customers very, very seriously.

5. Our customers REALLY are right.

6. Solving a problem at our expense is an important investment in our customers.

7. Customers must ALWAYS be respected and treated accordingly.

8. We want NO unhappy customers. We will do whatever it takes to make ALL our customers satisfied and happy with our service.

9. We respond quickly to all customer communications.

10. The way in which we solve every customer-service problem has crucial long-term ramifications not only on customer loyalty but ultimately on the success of our organization.

> "If your failure rate is one in a million, what do you tell that one customer?...When it comes to service, we treat every customer as if he or she is one in a million."
>
> IBM Advertisement

REVIEW OF STAGE V

This stage suggests four action plans for involving your customer-service team(s) in the problem-solving process. Each action plan promotes a proactive, rather than a reactive, approach to solving customer-service problems.

ACTION PLAN 1:

You can create a *SUPPORTIVE CLIMATE FOR SOLVING CUSTOMER-SER-VICE PROBLEMS* by utilizing proven techniques for reducing techniques for reducing resistance to change among your customer-service team members.

ACTION PLAN 2:

You can use your customer-service team(s) to *IDENTIFY AREAS OF STRENGTH AS WELL AS WEAKNESS* in your service delivery systems. The "Customer Service Assessment Scale" is designed to facilitate this process.

ACTION PLAN 3:

You can make your customer-service team(s) *A RESOURCE FOR IMPROVING SERVICE* by implementing brainstorming method to generate the best possible solutions for improving your customer-service delivery systems.

ACTION PLAN 4:

You can *TURN CUSTOMER PROBLEMS AND COMPLAINTS INTO OPPOR-TUNITIES TO STRENGTHEN TIES WITH YOUR CUSTOMERS* by replacing a knee-jerk reaction to customer complaints with a proactive response. View customer complaints as "luscious golden opportunities."

Note: When you succeed at implementing this action plan, you are coming full circle in the customer-service management process. In Action Plan 4 you are doing nothing less than *DEVELOPING A BETTER UNDERSTANDING OF YOUR CUSTOMER.*

YOUR ACTION PLAN FOR STAGE V

> THE CUSTOMER-SERVICE MANAGEMENT PROCESS IS, INDEED, A NEVER-ENDING SEQUENCE OF ENLIGHTENED MANAGEMENT ACTIONS.

After reviewing the four action plans suggested for creating a proactive problem-solving approach in your operation, what are YOU going to do NOW to put them into practice? Write your brief action plan in the space provided.

_____

_____

_____

_____

_____

_____

_____

_____

_____

_____

YOUR ACTION PLAN FOR THE COMPLETE CUSTOMER-SERVICE MANAGEMENT CYCLE

It is now time to review the actions plans you developed for each of the five stages of the customer-service management cycle. Take each plan and combine it with the others to create a single document. You now have a TOTAL PLAN OF ACTION that has been custom designed by you. It is now ready to be put into gear.

> *YOU ARE NOW HEADED IN THE RIGHT DIRECTION WITH A CLEAR SENSE OF PURPOSE AND A THOROUGH UNDERSTANDING OF WHAT IS NECESSARY TO CREATE QUALITY CUSTOMER SERVICE A REALITY IN YOUR OPERATION. ALL YOU HAVE TO DO NOW IS DO IT!*

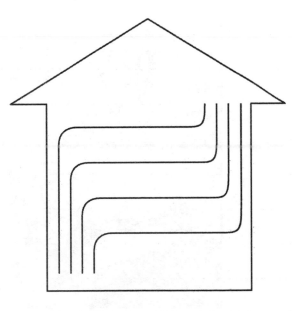

GOOD LUCK!

ADDITIONAL TRAINING PROGRAMS OFFERED THROUGH ARAMARK

World Class Service

World Class Patient Service

ARAMARK Academy - Guest Focus

Telephone Doctor (for ARAMARK Uniform Services employees)

For more information about these programs, please contact your Human Resources professional.

Nitgh
Nithesh.Bhandari@gmail.com.

Now Available From

Books•Videos•CD-ROMs•Computer-Based Training Products

Subject Areas Include:

Management

Human Resources

Communication Skills

Personal Development

Sales/Marketing

Finance

Coaching and Mentoring

Customer Service/Quality

Small Business and Entrepreneurship

Training

Life Planning

Writing

VERM